A HISTORY OF ROCHFORD

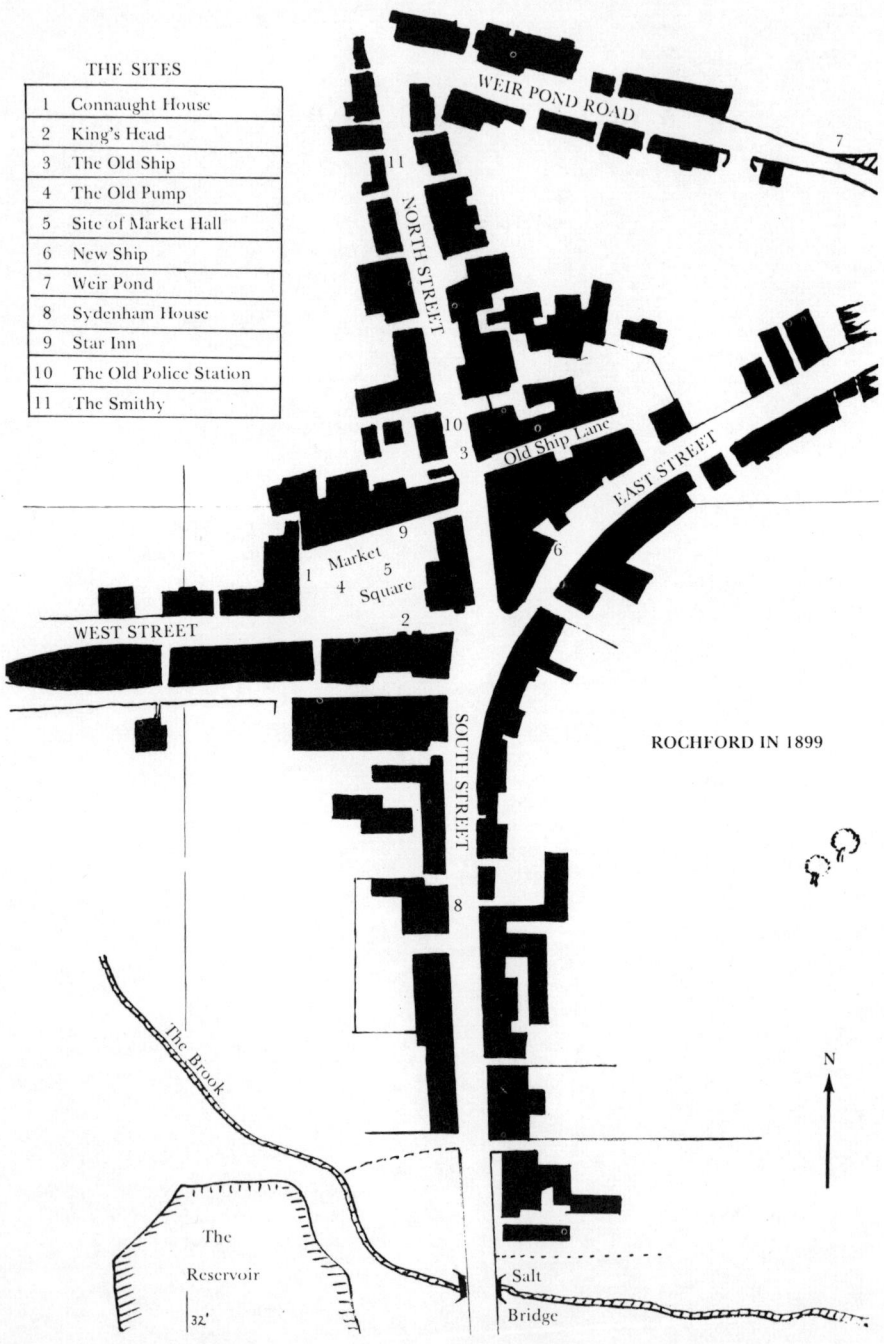

A History of Rochford

by

L. R. CRYER

with drawings by
JOHN H. FOUNTAIN

PHILLIMORE

1978
Published by
PHILLIMORE & CO., LTD.,
London and Chichester

Head Office: Shopwyke Hall,
Chichester, Sussex, England

ISBN 0 85033 249 4

© L. R. Cryer, 1978

Printed in Great Britain by
UNWIN BROTHERS LIMITED
at the Gresham Press, Old Woking, Surrey

To Kay, for all her understanding

CONTENTS

Chapter		Page
1	Rochford and Its Hundred	1
	The Hundred, the Town, the Bridges	
2	The Centre of Rochford	8
	The Market, the Market Hall, Connauaght House, the Martyrdom	
3	Rochford Hall	14
	The Hall, the Dovecote	
4	The Lawless Court	22
	The Court, King's Hill Cottages	
5	Water	27
	The Brook, the Pumps, the Town Hall	
6	Agriculture	33
	The Soil, the Crops, Superstitions, Wages	
7	The Two Fires	37
	The 1884 Fire, the Mafeking Celebrations	
8	Religion	40
	Rochford Church, Presbyterians, Congregationals, Wesleyans, Baptists, the Peculiar People	
9	The Banks	51
	Early Banks, Barclays, Westminster	
10	The Schools	54
	Early Schools, National School, the Vicarage School, Nuns' School, Today's Schools	
11	The Industries of Rochford	62
	The Potash, the Gas Works, the Brick and Tile Fields, the Mills	
12	The Traders of Rochford	69
	Tailors, Drapers, Ironmongers, Saddlers, Blacksmiths, Wheelwrights, Candlemakers	

Chapter		Page
13	More Rochford Traders Butchers, Bakers, Grocers, Watchmakers, Bootmakers, Plumbers	77
14	The Two Murders Mrs. E. Hunt, Mrs. Wilkes	85
15	The Police Early Custodians and Cases, the Essex Force, Notable Police, the old Police Station	88
16	The Workhouse, the Almshouses, and Other Charities Early Provision for Vagrants, the Union of 1837	94
17	Transport and Roads The Coaches, the Railway, Travel by Water, Roads, the Turnpike, 'Turnpike Cottage'	103
18	Some Rochford Personalities and Families Farmer Meeson, Dr. Asplin, Francis the printer, the Bishops, the Priors, the Gregsons, Arthur Harrington, William Kernott, the Mosses	113
19	The Farms The Hall Farm, Great Doggett's, Swaine's, Coombe's, Great Brays, Evan's, Golden Cross, Gusted Hall, Pelham's, New England, Flemings, Blatches, Tapes, Pipehorns	123
20	Old Buildings in Rochford The Moot House, the China Store, 'Freeman's Cottages', 'Acacia House', 'Ash Cottage', 'Vine Cottage', 'The Lavenders', 'The Hollies', 'Enigma House', 'The Court House', 'Osborne House', 'The Lawn', the Court House, 'Malting Cottages'	135
21	Postal Services Early post arrangements, the postmasters	143
22	Miss Tawke Hunting recollections; her home	149

Chapter		Page
23	The Inns of Rochford - - - - - -	152
	Old Ship, New Ship, Marlborough Head, Vernon's Head, King's Head, Horse and Groom, Rose and Crown, White Horse, The Cock, Three Ashes, Anne Boleyn, Golden Lion, and others	
24	The Hospitals - - - - - -	159
	Noble's Green, Sweyne's, Sutton Ford Bridge	
25	Population - - - - - - - -	162
	Hearth Tax, 1671; Population, 1801–1971	
26	Conclusion - - - - - - - -	169
	Bibliography - - - - - - -	171
	References - - - - - - - -	173
	Index - - - - - - - - -	186

LIST OF ILLUSTRATIONS

Plates *Between pages 32 and 33*

Frontis. Rochford in 1899
1. The Pump
2. The Whispering Post
3. Custom House, Weir Pond Road
4. The Old Cannon, dated 1813
5. The Photographer, North Street
6. The Old Workhouse, Southend Road
7. The Post Office, West Street
8. Market Alley
9. Rochford Hall, north side
10. The Old Barn, Hall Road
11. Old Post Office, 1880
12. Rochford Market
13. The *Rose and Crown*
14. Hartley's the Saddler, founded 1777

Line drawings by Sarah Major and John H. Fountain

Between pages 112 and 113

1. Market Hall by Sarah Major
2. The Cottages, Union Lane
3. Malting Cottages, Weir Pond Road
4. Market Square
5. Front View of Rochford Hall
6. Back View of Rochford Hall
7. Rochford Hall; one of the octagonal towers
8. The Old Barn, Doggett's Farm
9. Rochford Church, Hall Road

10   The nine-bay Barn, Great Doggett's
11   The Old Moot House, 17 South Street
12   Sydenham House School, South Street
13   The Old Mill House, West Street
14   The site of the *Horse and Groom* inn, Southend Road

Figures in the text   *page*
1a   Plan of Rochford Hall, with dove-cote, 1796   ..   15
1b   Plan of Rochford Hall   18
2   The dove-cote, Rochford Hall, drawing of 1883   20
3   Poem 'The Poor Old Pump', 1902   31
4a   Rochford academy: Boy's inventory   55
4b   Rochford academy: Bill of 1828   56
4c   King's Hill School Prospectus 1888   56
5   Handbill of the Haberdashery, c. 1885   83
6a   Menus for the Workhouse, 1843 and 1893   ..   96
6b   Dinner to mark the end of the Workhouse, 1930   99
7a   The Rochford Turnpike, 1796   109
7b   Road to the Lawn and Gusted Hall, 1862   ..   109
8   Dr. Aspin's farm, the Garlands, 1809   114
9   Key Plan, Rochford Hall Estate, 1867   124
10a Essex Postal System, 1828   145
10b Postmarks for 1823/4 and 1841   145

ACKNOWLEDGMENTS

MY THANKS are due to so many people that it seems a pity I can but mention a few. Apart from facts gleaned from the sources listed, I had much help from the staff and documents at the Essex Records Office and from the librarians of Southend Library, the Guildhall, London, and the British Museum.

Perhaps my greatest sources of information, however, have been the senior citizens of Rochford itself. I have recorded the help from Harry Chapman, now in his 99th year. His background, his father was steward at Rochford Hall, his historical leanings and experience as clerk of various works were of real worth. Jack Topsfield, blacksmith, 'Chick' Robinson, painter, Mr. Roughton, cycles and motor agent, and Mr. Bloomfield were also invaluable.

Brigadier R. Bryers and the late Miss Coombes gave help for the chapter on schools, the Records Department of the Post Office assisted me with details of mail, services, and servants and the Divisional Manager, Eastern Region of British Railways, gave me facts on transport.

To the archivist, Essex Record Office, my special thanks for allowing me to quote from their publication, No. 56, *Elizabethan Life—Disorder,* by F. G. Emmison. I was encouraged by S. C. Harris, P. Whittingham, W. Squier, and E. Bull, whose help and information contributed to the text.

Mrs. Nia Clasby (M.A., Cantab) very kindly read through my notes and suggested several additions and alterations, for which I was most grateful.

My thanks would not be complete without mention of my former secretary, Mrs. E. M. Cooper, who typed much of my earlier notes, to the late Mrs. M. Fletcher, who carried on the task, and Mrs. G. Chase, who completed it.

To all these and many others, who gave me their time, helped me with information, gave or loaned me pictures, documents and books, I express my gratitude. In particular, Fig. 1b is taken from the Royal Commission on Historical Monuments, S.E. Essex Inventory, 1923, which is reproduced with the permission of the Controller, H.M.S.O. Their help enabled me to finish a task that would have been so much more difficult.

L. R. Cryer

FOREWORD

I FIRST BECAME interested in the history of Rochford in 1965 when I made the acquaintance of Harry Chapman. His father had worked at the great Hall and had passed on many stories to his son. When I last saw him in 1971 Harry was then 94, with a remarkable memory stretching back over the years, and he fostered in me his liking for the area.

When I carried on my own enquiries I was surprised to find that nobody had written a story of the town itself, the nearest perhaps being the *History of the Rochford Hundred,* by Philip Benton, but as that was dated 1867 I felt sure much happened in the intervening years that was of interest and that would be lost in the march of time were it not recorded.

So I began to set down my information from the wealth of materials I had gathered, for from this small town which even by the year 1921 could boast but a mere 2,000 people, much had happened. On its outskirts was the beginning of a great forest stretching on to Rayleigh and Hadleigh, wherein a king hunted before riding on to visit his paramour here; it saw the beginning of a new religion; its centre, the Market Square, which enjoyed rights for over 700 years, saw many a sight, including two fires and a martyrdom, and within its locality two widely differing murders were perpretrated. So there was much to write about, and as the pages turn perhaps many incidents will remain alive because of the telling.

Chapter One

ROCHFORD AND ITS HUNDRED

ROCHFORD WAS THE chief town of Rochford Hundred to which it gave its name. Coller[1] said there were 19 hundreds in Essex with some other divisions. There had been much controversy over the word Hundred, for whilst Stubbs[2] said it was certain that in some instances it was a hundred hides of land, Doris Shelton[3] understood it to mean a division of land for local government from Anglo-Saxon England. Ralph Arnold,[4] in his turn was more definite and expressed the view that by the end of the 10th century, every shire in the land had been divided into small administrative districts called Hundreds, with a court whose president was generally a reeve or steward from the nearest royal estates. Allen[5] subscribed to the view that Alfred began the system where the meaning was one of jurisdiction over a hundred men, and delivered the opinion that these Hundreds were given responsibility for the pursuit of fugitives and thieves, and Arnold wrote that Canute in one of his laws stated that every freeman, if he were 12 years old . . . be brought into a hundred or tithing.[6] On the other hand Munro Chadwick[7] maintained that the evidence of the existence of a Hundred went back as far as the laws of King Edmund.

Whatever view was taken as to the meaning, it was certain that the Rochford Hundred was a very important one. Its cereal crops, its meat and wool, its mustard and potatoes were all a vital part in the existence of the city of London, from which it was only some two score miles by road and could be reached by water, by boat and barge.

The Hundred was bounded on the south by the Thames, on the east side by the North Sea, on the west by the Hundred of Barstable, and to the north for much of its part, by the river Crouch, wherein it contained some 60,000 acres of land said Benton.[8] It derived its name from the river Roche and a ford existed on the site of the Salt bridge which separated it from the parish of Eastwood in early times. It contained 26 parishes and had a length of 10-17 miles from east to west, and a width of seven miles wherein it had some of the best soil in the country—and some of the worst.

The west and central portions were well wooded, Benton[9] declared and, indeed, there was a chain of woodlands extending from Hadleigh through Rayleigh and Hawkwell to the borders of Rochford. Bayne[10] affirmed that in 1380 the Earl of Oxford held the Bailwick of the Rochford Hundred on condition that . . . 'he kept at his own cost and charge, the fences and lodges of the King's parks at Rayleigh, Hadleigh and Thundersley in good repair'. This royal hunting ground continued right on through to the reign of Henry VIII, who made frequent journeys to Hadleigh castle, to hunt the stags and wild boar in Rayleigh park, and from here he came to woo Anne Boleyn[11] at Rochford Hall. Benton expressed the opinion that even as late as 1805,[12] the woods still amounted to 2,000 acres hereabouts.

The south part of the region was flat and from want of drainage and lack of freshwater, was formerly subject to malaria, ague, mildew, and stinking fogs. The low parts were continually subject to inundation, especially in 1881[13], whilst who can forget the memories of the 1953 floods at Canvey and elsewhere on the east coast. Yet Norden in

1539[14] said the shire deserved the title of Goshen, a land that flowed with milk and honey, a land that grew oats abundantly: so it certainly had its extremes.

The early inhabitants were the Kimmerians and Celts, afterwards called the Cymry[15] who dwelt in underground caves and passages called argillas. Traces of their existence were found near Wakering Hall when digging for brick earth. They used woad on their bodies and fought with axes and javelins, as well as the bow and arrow. They were ruled by chiefs and also priests called Druids. Later when the Romans came they found the Trinobantes people[16] in and around Essex, and it was Boadicea from one of their tribes, the Iceni, who attempted to overthrow the invaders. When the Huns and Goths finally defeated the Romans in Europe the invaders were recalled to help defend Rome. This was around 420, and it left the way clear for the Picts and Scots to ravage the country from the north. So much so that the Britons bribed the Saxons to come over in 449 A.D. to repel them. Having done so, these second invaders stayed, but the Saxons did not take Essex until around 530 A.D., and formed the kingdom of East Saxa, which they held for nearly 600 years, although for much of the latter part of their rule they were beset by the Danes, a struggle which finally ended in the Battle of Assandune, with Canute winning the day. A compromise was reached by which England was halved between them, a state of affairs that continued more or less unchanged until the coming of the Normans.

The Hundred court of Rochford was annexed to the Manor of Rayleigh and thereafter granted by the King to high personages, beginning after the conquest with Suene, a Saxon of some Norman descent who assisted William at his coming. He made Rayleigh castle his chief seat to administer the feudal system.

Rochford was mentioned in Domesday under the name Rochefort as having a mill and was held by Alured of Suene and by a freeman in the time of King Edward for a manor and for two and a half hides. From this manor of Rochford came that of Guested Hall and likewise the reputed manor of Doggetts and Coombes said Benton.[17] The town was bounded on the south by a small stream which led into the river Roche and which generally divided it from the parish of Eastwood, whilst to the west it was bordered by Hawkwell and Rayleigh. Part of Ashingdon road formed its northern boundary and it turned into Golden Cross road as far as the end of Great Doggett's farm, after which the parish of Little Stambridge was reached.

When it became the capital of the Hundred it took up trade with London and so came to be a centre itself with a market which was of ancient standing for Sir Guy de Rochford had a market and fair in 1247.[18] He was summoned in 1258 to show why he claimed the right to a wreck at sea. He made good his title to this privilege and to the right to hold a market every Tuesday and a fair yearly for a full three days at Whitsun. At his death in 1274 he held, among other estates, in the town of Rochford a messuage with garden, 160 acres of arable land, a park with 32 acres of woodland in it, assize rents, seven acres of meadow with the right of patronage of the church of Rochford, and also a windmill in the town.[19] After his death, by gift and grant, by buying and selling, the lord of the manor of Rochford controlled almost half of the land in Rochford as the great sale of the estate in 1867 showed.

From early times the centre of the town was formed by the crossing of four streets named simply after the main points of the compass, but they did not run in quite that orderly fashion, for East Street was not at right angles to

West Street, but began near the top end of South Street, to bear left in a north-easterly direction before it finally joined North Street via Weir Pond Road. By the end of the 18th century, Rochford could be entered also by way of Hall Road, coming from the direction of Hawkwell. Sir John Tylney Long of the Hall, before his death in 1784 had altered the road which had come up Potash Hill and on to the back of the Hall before entering the town. There is reason to believe it crossed the stream by way of stepping-stones, at a spot today between the point where the new by-pass begins at West Street and the present road up to the railway station. About 1775 he began to straighten the road so that it came from Ark Lane on down to the town, so passing the front of the Hall, and he then made a new structure in 1777 over the brook hereafter called the Town bridge. This was at the very end of West Street or Church Street, as the latter part is often called. Although renewed several times since, for on 5 October 1864 it was repaired by Codd the builder, and as recently as 1970 when it was widened for car and lorry traffic, the old plaque is still preserved on one of the sides though its three arches have now become one. It was about this time that Tylney Long planted a fine avenue of oak and ash trees for his new road, and in so doing placed a £10 fine on each tree, to prevent them from being cut down. Sad to say, such was their fate in later years, but the penalty was not enforced.

Another bridge connected with the town has already been mentioned, the Salt bridge situated at the beginning of South Street. In 1966, a new by-pass, called Bradley Way, was begun close by, which opened on 13 November 1967.

This allowed traffic, after leaving the bridge, to avoid the awkward crossing at the top of South Street, where it joined North Street, or worse, where it turned sharp left to enter the Market Square into West Street, by filtering it off left and causing it to enter the town into the bottom of West Street and then turning it into Ashingdon Road. It was on 29 June 1967 that workmen who were demolishing the old bridge came across traces of an even earlier structure. I was passing soon after and obtained a piece of this old wood, quite sound, if weathered. The foreman indicated to me his belief that it was perhaps a part of a raft on which an older bridge was built. The brickwork, he continued, was bonded with a limestone mix. In July 1709[20] at a meeting in the town, the repairs that had previously been ordered for the bridge were arranged to stand over owing to the heavy flooding that had then occurred, whilst again on 28 April 1764[21] repairs costing £11 19s. 7d. were made. Then in 1772,[22] the Weld brothers were asked to build a new bridge. This they did with William making the iron framing and doing the brickwork, and Daniel all the necessary woodworking. A feature of the bill for the total of £236 was that it contained a credit for selling off an old iron structure, i.e., a previous bridge. Theirs followed the customary three-arch principal, perhaps an indication also that the stream was then much wider than today, where one arch suffices. Their structure was restored in 1830 and again in 1904, this latter when more elm piles were found, said Harry Chapman, who told me that two of the workmen for Norden the builder made tool chests from the old wood, although it was quite black with age. It was said to have taken its name from the fact that this was the limit of tidal or salt water carried up from Broomhills, a theory well supported by the following incident: in August 1968 a cod weighing 10lbs. was caught by a pupil from the nearby primary school at a spot between the two bridges, thus being well clear of the supposed boundary.

A third bridge with some association with Rochford was the Sutton Ford bridge that stood about half a mile down the Sutton Road and which was built after a much older ford there had become dangerous. A petition[23] signed by some 52 people, which included the names of J. Kersteman of Wakering, Golden Prentice, who had the Maltings, John Harriott, William Cockerton, farmer, Robert Salmon, shopkeeper, J. Lodwick at Rochford Hall, and Dr. Thomas Swaine, dated 1772, showed there was much concern over its bad state. John Harriott (1754–1816) was a magistrate for Rochford between the years 1782 and 1793. He was also the instigator of the Thames River Police. An estimate for gravel, posts and railings costing £54 was made in 1772[24], but as it was surveyed again on 19 April 1784 when the estimate for bridge fencing and some road levelling was put at £349, it seemed the most likely date. Despite the cost of flattening the road, there was still a large hump on the crown of the bridge which bore a strong resemblance to the old pack-horse type. It was restored again in 1902, when the cement walls were removed, to be replaced by ironwork tracery which carried two central bosses with the date inscribed.

Chapter Two

THE CENTRE OF ROCHFORD

The Market

IF ROCHFORD derived its name from the river, the town surely got its life, not to say its livelihood, from the Square, for here everything of importance happened. The Great Fire, as it was called, of 1884, the bonfire made to celebrate the relief of Mafeking, the site of the old pump of 1820 with its queues of people for the drawing of water twice daily, the sale of wool from the Market Hall, market day on Thursday, with a cattle sale every other week, the scene of a martyrdom,[1] the starting place for coaches prior to 1823/4 (after which South End was the beginning point), the spot where fairs were held twice yearly, where circuses, like Biddulf's showed, where the German silver band marched and counter-marched, the place of assembly of local organisations, such as the Foresters: all had their sights and sounds for the Square.

From its very early origin, the market had its ups and downs. Coller[2] confirmed Benton, and put its date at 1247, in the reign of Henry III. We know it lapsed in later years since Benton[3] recorded its re-establishment by John Harriott, 'that energetic reformer'. It must have stopped again, for on 16 February 1905[4] it was renewed, and again we find from the Council minutes the market was to re-start on 28 May 1914 for the sale of livestock, when the market rights were given over by James Tabor, J.P., as lord of the manor of Rochford Hall, to Hilliard the auctioneer. Once more it went out of business, for an investigation was held on 13 February 1925 to decide if it was worth resurrection. It must have been successful since the market continued on until 1959. Reasons for its stopping prior to Harriott's time were hard to find, but for its decease in later years grounds were evident. The rapid rise in the growth of South End, henceforth to be known as Southend, following a Royal accolade, and later still the upsurge in the population and prestige of near neighbours such as Rayleigh took away the commerce and trade, so Rochford's market languished. The railway, too, must have taken a large share of the buying and selling away.

The Market Square is really an oblong[5] of approximately eight poles by seven, situated centrally in the town on the north side of West Street, and quite close to the other three main streets. In the early days there was keen competition for its shops. Even today rivalry has remained, for with the loss of the market in 1959 has come a great rush of motor traffic to prove that its popularity may only have waned.

Yet in the last 10 years many changes have taken place hereabouts, not the least being the great alteration on its east side. Here there were two long-established businesses. At the one end closest to the alley, Bartons, the bakers, have a shop, but it was in this trade from 1825, if not before. There are many photographs and postcards with the sign and that date over the door still in the possession of Rochfordians.

On the other end the ousted grocer was the firm of E. Shelley, there for half a century, with others in like pursuit before them. The bakery and the other shops up to Shelley had thatched roofs. D. G. Macleod[6] examined the whole row during the demolition in November 1961. Of the grocery concern he believed it had five constructional phases with the extreme end a two-storey double-bayed building with leaded light windows having queen struts with axis north-south, probably built in the early 16th century.

The Market Hall

Christy[7] said the hall was built in 1707 of wood and plaster and had a tiled roof with a turret of open timbers containing the town bell. Benton said it was a model of the Cinque Port Court House. The roof was pyramidal with the apex cut away for the bell-cote, while in the wooden dormer a clock was installed for the benefit of the townsfolk. It occupied about four perches of ground[8] and was situated in the upper part of the square. It had two storeys with the lower part containing a series of open porches in one half, the other being enclosed and used for a variety of purposes; at one time a gaol, a barber's shop, and a stall for cattle, whilst the open part was used as a covered market for the sale of cheese, butter, eggs, etc. It also served as a shelter in bad weather, and later housed the first parish fire engine. In fact the list seemed never-ending, for Rev. J. Wise, wrote to William Bullock, steward for the Manor, whose property the Market Square was, on 21 December 1809, asking on whose authority someone had converted the lower portion as a residence.

The top portion was used as a wool store and distribution centre for the district around, especially Canvey, which was noted for its sheep-rearing qualities. Messrs. Johns of Baddow, near Chelmsford, were its tenants for many years, advertising sales of wool by using the town bell. Later it served more mundane purposes, becoming a general storehouse for all the things the market needed.

By 1809 the spire at least was in a dangerous condition, and the clock face was almost invisible for dirt. So on 20 March 1810[9] Wise again wrote to William Bullock and asked if something could be done to improve matters, stating a sum of £24 was required for repairs to the turret. The Manor was not prepared to help in this, and no wonder, since it was charging a peppercorn rent of 1s. per annum. This appeal having failed, he wrote to a man named White for help, some three months later, but no aid was given. The building grew progressively worse, and finally, in 1861[10] it was pulled down. By this time it was a real public danger and pieces had fallen away in many parts. The bell was later used in the Corn Exchange for their cereal trade, but later it was taken to the museum at Prittlewell Priory. I believe the clock was last in the possession of the owner of Purdey's farm.

It was a great coincidence that whilst looking round the outhouses of a wooden bungalow called 'Sunnyside', in Back Lane, in the year 1966, I found a piece of elm about 11ft. 5in. long, and four inches square, with the date March 1861 chalked on it. The building belonged to A. Ling, the cabinet-maker, who built it all of wood, save for its brick chimney. He had assisted in the demolition, and no doubt feeling the wood could come in useful, had stored it in the place he used as a workshop. Its length suggested it was one of the rafters or a supporting post.

Connaught House

This is situated on the west side of the Square, taking the whole of that side save for the two ends. On the north end lies 'Fernside', a small house, now numbered 32, which lies back from the main building-line of Connaught House. In it lived Harry Sparrow when he was an apprentice for Simmons the vet., who himself lived in 'Vine Cottage', West Street. On the other end, where the street narrows, lay a shop that had housed a variety of trades. It was an implement stores, first for Meeson, then for Maldon ironworks, but later James the florist had it, and more recently it changed hands very quickly to become a betting office, a corner cafe, and a calling-on spot for taxis.

Connaught House was built in Georgian style in the latter part of the 18th century. From various facts and with help from Harry Chapman, I estimated the date of building as 1770. Mr. Conder Halsey, whose mother owned the house later, agreed with this date. It had a fine doorway with Tuscan columns which can still be seen. It is used as part of the annexe of the Rochford Hospital, mainly as a residence for aged people.

It was built by Collis, a man of Irish descent who was supposed to have used his winnings from a lottery for this purpose. Could it have been something like the Irish sweepstake? He was followed in turn by four solicitors, the first being James Vanderzee, who was there in 1793. Then came Michael Comport, whose name appeared in 1823/4 as the clerk to the Rochford Hundred Union or Workhouse. He resigned this office on 16 March 1859, and left the district. William Gregson, born 28 April 1842, came next, he being the second son of William Gregson of 'The Cottage', Stroud Green, since demolished. He began as an auctioneer and land agent when he lived at 'Fir Tree House', East Street. It was from there that he married Mary, the daughter of Edward Jackson of the Rochford bank, and they began their domestic life at Connaught House. The other brother, Frederick, also a solicitor, lived at 'The Lavenders', in the

The Centre of Rochford   13

lower part of West Street. William's name is first recorded
in 1832 and continued up to 1886. Last of the lawyers
to reside here was A. J. Arthy, who was registered from 1878
to 1908. Round about the early part of 1895, Charlotte
Horlock came to Rochford, with a hundred men from the
Greenwich Union, and she purchased the house and rented
two others; but perhaps its most interesting owner was
Edward John Halsey, born in 1875. He married Joan, born
1885, the daughter of Rankin, the Stambridge miller, in
1909. It was in 1916 that they came to live here. He was a
shipping manager for the Hudson Bay Fur Trapping Company, who had offices in Great Thorrington Street, London.
After he died on 3 July 1934 his wife remained here until
1940. It then stayed empty, until bought by Southend
Corporation in 1946 as part of their hospital complex.

The Martyrdom
On 10 June 1555 the Square was the scene of the execution
of John Simson,[11] a husbandman of Great Wigborough,
near Clacton. He had been condemned for his religious
beliefs, together with a Rayleigh man, named John Ardeley.
Both men answered their examiner, Bishop Bonner, in the
Palace at Fulham so boldly, especially Simson, that the
Bishop grew angry and exclaimed, 'Have him away, have
him away!' Bonner then had to run away from the crowd
to his apartments. They offered Queen Mary all their
belongings in return for freedom of worship, but every
plea was rejected. So they were taken back to their respective towns and burnt at the stake in the markets. Singularly,
it was not until 26 May 1956 that a plaque to Simson's
memory was put up on the east side of the Square. It was
removed when the whole of that side was rebuilt in 1961
and placed just above head-height in the alley.

Chapter Three

ROCHFORD HALL

THIS OLD BUILDING lay near the west end of the church, and, like it, there were doubts as to its date. Benton[1] said one tradition named James, Earl of Ormond, as its builder and that it was burnt down in its early years. He gave another fire here the date $c.$ 1760[2] and said it remained in its ruinous state for some time. Then the windows were modernised and the red brickwork was plastered over. Whatever its date it was in 1515 that Bullen of Norfolk acquired it for his services to the King, and we know that 10 years later he was created Viscount Rochford. It was at the Hall that Anne, his daughter, grew up. Coller put it very well when he said, '. . . this old house in which she was cradled, the grounds and gardens where her young feet chased the butterfly with the church hard by where perhaps she lisped her early prayers'.[3] It was from here that she was appointed maid of honour to the then Queen, Katherine of Aragon. This was in 1522, but she was soon back home, as she formed an early attachment to Lord Percy for which she was temporarily banished from court. She was then only twenty. She returned to London in 1527 and it seemed likely that it was at this time she caught the attention of Henry, who pursued her, even to her home. It was in 1533 that he married her, albeit secretly, since his divorce was not then complete. The house was then quite small, for it was not until the Earls of Warwick came into possession that the

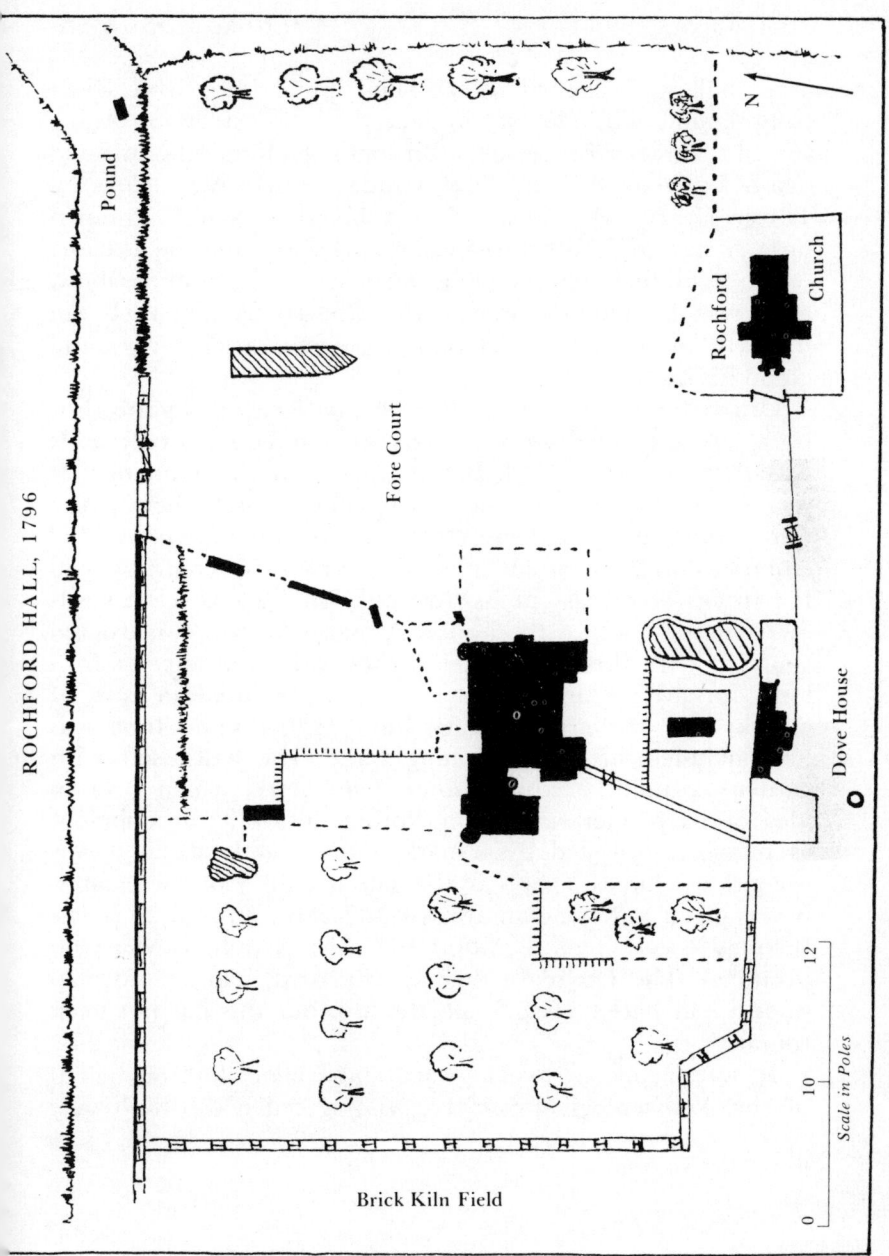

Fig. 1a Plan of Rochford Hall, with dove-cote, 1796

great hall was planned. Alas! Their grand ideas were never fully completed; almost, in fact, like the story of Anne, for but three short years after her wedding, she suffered death by being beheaded at midday on 19 May 1536 on Tower Green. Her husband and his friends had trumped up a charge of adultery against her. Benton[4] quoted a report which said that her unfeeling husband, with hounds about him, was impatiently waiting for the Tower gun to boom its awful note to tell him of her passing, so that he could go on his hunt.

Originally the Hall was to have had four courtyards, but the plan appended showed only two were constructed. It was then partly moated, but no traces of this remained. It was a two-storey building with gabled roof where attics were constructed for the staff. A feature was its twisted chimneys with an abundance of waterspouts. Tradition said the bricks were cast in its own pits, only a few score yards away at the back of the house. A high wall was constructed round it with slits some three inches wide, and about a foot long for arrows and blunderbusses to be used in case of attack. The steward's cottage built at the same time was not included in the encircling wall.[5] The hall itself with gardens around, occupied some eight acres, which gave an idea of its former size. John Norden in 1539[6] described it as being surrounded by a park and certainly when it was bought by James Tabor at the sale in 1867[7] of the estates, it was given as having an area of 407 acres 3 roods 22 poles. Its new owner paid £25,000 for this. Arthur Tawke who occupied 'The Lawn' further up the road, had an old map of the hall dated 1688,[8] said Benton, but this has not been found.

It was inspected by Hayward and Chancellor[9] on behalf of the Archaeological Society, who agreed it was built over a long period of time: in fact the former suggested a date of 1500. In 1877,[10] it was surveyed again by H. Prigg, from Bury, who used a walking stick to take brief and rather rough measurements. The west wing which he checked more thoroughly had walls of three feet thickness, which dimension he assigned to all the others, but his findings only included some of the doors and windows. In the inner angles of the building were octagonal turrets which had inner spiral staircases. Harry Chapman told me the stairways were cut from solid blocks of oak. Today only parts of the east wing remain. Benton[11] wrote that even in his time an entire room with upper chambers had been pulled down, and in the mid-19th century a further part of the south-east corner had to be demolished. The front portion of all that remains is today let to the Rochford Hundred Golf Club.

Reasons for its rapid decline were not hard to find. By 1750 it had passed into the hands of John, Earl Tylney, of Wanstead House, who died in 1784. His nephew, James, inherited it until his death in 1794.[12] Then it fell to his son, Sir James Tylney Long, who died unmarried and under age, a sickly youth, in 1805. His sister, Catherine, succeeded him, and on 14 March 1812[13] married William Wellesley Pole. The ceremony was a foretaste of what was to come, for it was a magnificent affair, as Benton recorded. Her husband in the space of the next 10 years had run through her large fortune, so much so that most of the estate, including Wanstead House had to be pulled down, and its contents and all building materials sold. This had been erected in 1715[14] by Sir Richard Child, at a cost of more than £360,000, which gave a clear indication of the total disaster. The growing crops of the farms at Rochford Hall and Swaines were sold by auction by Jacksons the auctioneers, of Hertford, in July 1822. The sale included

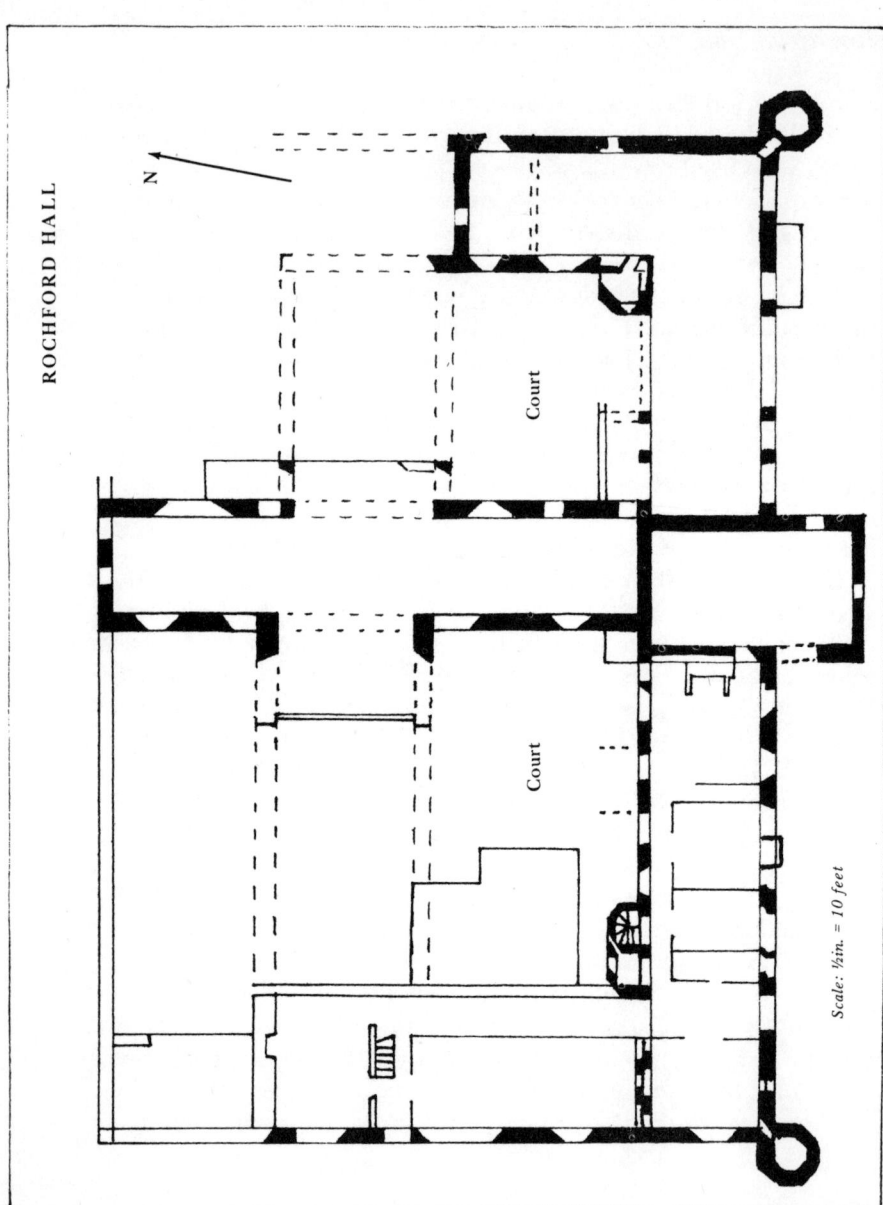

Fig. 1b Plan of Rochford Hall

Rochford Hall

live and dead stock, household furniture, and other effects.

Rochford Hall was not sold, which was perhaps a pity, as it suffered under a number of tenant farmers who paid scant heed to a building not theirs. So we find the families of Slys, Wright (who failed as a farmer), the Harrisons, Wilsons, and the Lodwicks here. John of that name was here in 1835-45[15] and was followed in 1848[16] by J. Tabor, who purchased it, as mentioned, in 1867.[17]

The Dovecote

To the south of the hall, in a small meadow, just outside the enclosing wall, was this building. Just beyond it lay the brick-fields spoken of (no wonder it, too, was of brick construction). It was one of the earliest built in England, and though it was first written of in 1620, its date was *c.* 1560. The colombary was circular in shape as the drawing attached showed, which made it of unusual design, there being only seven such others built, while it was unique in that it was the only one known to have been thatched. This roofing material continued up to within five feet of its conical top, which was then open save for the rafters, so allowed easy access to the birds. Its walls were three feet thick at the base, and it had a diameter of 40 feet. Inside were 10 rows of partitions, so that it could have housed up to 300 fowls.

Long before its demise it suffered indignities, for in its later days it became a store-house, and a barn for cattle, while Tabor had used it both for a piggery and for broody hens. Again, like the hall, it was seldom, if ever, repaired, and when it was struck by lightning in 1888,[18] only five years after my illustration was made, this and its parlous condition, completed its downfall.

DOVE-COTE, ROCHFORD HALL, ESSEX.

Fig. 2

D. Smith further told of a letter written by a Mrs. Jackson[19] of Rochford, to a friend, in which said of the Dovecote '... it was originally fitted with a trapdoor which could be opened and shut by means of a pulley with ropes or a chain attached to the catch, to let the birds out'. Mrs. F. Witham of Rayleigh,[20] whose father had been landlord of the *Horse and Groom* related the story of the payment of tithes for the parish of Eastwood to the bailiff of the Manor of Rochford Hall at this inn. She wrote that it was followed by a dinner at nearly six o'clock, when a feature of the meal was an enormous pigeon pie, the birds for which had been brought over from the hall dovecote by an old shepherd, who placed the game in the roomy side-pockets of his greatcoat. He would have walked across the meadow, then through the orchard and passed by the Wilderness, crossing a small stream, and so down a lane which today has houses on its sides and rejoices in the name of Rochford Hall Close.

Somewhat later, in 1926,[21] Sir Alfred Temple's book of verse had a poem called 'By Rochford Tower', with a couplet which ran,

> And the old Hall I know
> Its ruined dovecote and its bowers.

This truly was poetic licence, since the pigeon loft had gone some 40 years before, and as for the bower in the garden of the Hall it had gone long, long since.

These days we often hear the phrase 'keeping up with the Jones's', but it is important to remember these places were not just a show of wealth. They were generally attached to a feudal manor and could only be built by qualified people said Benton.[22] Their main purpose was to provide a source of fresh meat.

Chapter Four

THE LAWLESS COURT AND KING'S HILL

NO STORY OF Rochford would be complete without reference to this custom of which much has been written. It is safe to say that little was fact, much was odd, some was whimsical, and a great deal untrue. Its very source was in dispute, although 1620 seemed to have been its probable date of origin. Weever[1] in 1631 was the first who wrote about it, and he indicated Rayleigh as the earliest site. 'It was a singular custom', said Charnock[2] 'and occurred thus'. The lord of the manor came home late one night from foreign wars where he had been fighting. (Perhaps he was a mercenary?) He heard whispers coming from people near his house, so stopped to listen, whereupon he learned that his tenant farmers were plotting against him. Pretending not to have noticed, he made a noise to frighten them away and passed by.

As a penalty he ordered them to attend at midnight on the first Wednesday after Michaelmas, which was the unlawful or lawless hour. They were to parade with torches to light their way to the appointed spot. On arrival their names were called in a whisper and after reply they were to beat out their burning brands. Some authorities have probably added to the story, by the statement that the blackened ends were used to record their marks as a true sign of their presence. Others have written that the torches were struck out on a post. Certainly failure to attend or to have been late meant a fine. W. H. Black in 1869[3] and William Andrews in 1892[4] gave varying accounts of the custom which had then sunk to the level of a somewhat convivial occasion, for the walk to post was preceded by a grand dinner, with much drink to follow.

Benton[5] spoke of the original site in Rayleigh as being a mile or more from a public house, up a miry lane in a primitive state, a deplorable approach, he continued. It was transferred later, which was a great convenience, he proclaimed. This was done by the second Earl of Warwick since he had taken to residing at Rochford Hall. The word 'Lawlesse' occurred for the first time in 1676. Benton wrote that the existing rolls went no further back than 1758.[6] The Essex Record Office at Chelmsford have an account of the court, very much the worse for wear dated 1760.[7] At this place there is a further note of the court as held 10 October 1676 in the Manor of Rochford, alias Rochford Hall, where it was called the private establishment of Mary, Dowager Countess of Warwick, at a cross called the market cross.[8] The list of tenants,[9] 11 in number from around Rochford, had their individual rents recorded, the total being £5   13s. 2d. It further stated the court was held on the second day after Michaelmas at King's Hill, Rochford, where after calling the register, the steward adjourned to the *King's Head* inn, to await any latecomers, who were fined double their rent for non-appearance. I have been unable to find a reason for the site at King's Hill save that it was close to the centre of the town and the inn named. Undoubtedly it had the Whispering Post which again was a later tradition for Benton stated that the steward's rolls first mentioned it in 1772.[10] He went on to describe the post as being five feet high with the top spike shaped to resemble the flame of a candle. The date of the present post, he presumed, was 1867.

Assuredly the post remains today with that date incised on it, though the court no longer exists. This venerable post was made by the Allens, carpenters of Rochford, who had works in South Street. John, the father born in 1799, died on 18 February 1879.[11] Both he and William, his son, had a great reputation for good workmanship. Despite this, knowing what had happened to the hall in the Market Square, made me doubt very much that a post, even of oak, would have lasted, subject to the vagaries of the weather. Sure enough, when I examined it in 1970, at the back, quite close to the ground was a small brass plate recording its renewal in November 1935. Cyril Smoothy, whose father had lived at King's Hill, told me he had made the plate, which a man named Passfield, a carpenter working for F. J. Cook (who had made the new post) had screwed on for him. The latter had a workshop just beyond Salt Bridge. I must add that this post also was considerably eaten through at the base.

Morant[12] said the court was kept at King's Hill in the yard of a house kept by a gentleman called Crips, and later owned by Robert Hackshaw, a merchant of London. After that it was in the possession of John Buckle before a further Londoner, called Charles Taylor, held it. Documents about these folk have not been found, but I know it was owned by the elder Prior, Henry, who was here in 1870[13]-86[14] after which Mrs. S. Prior kept on the *New Ship* after her husband died. The property was conveyed to W. G. Smoothy on 7 September 1893, so presumably it was held by Punch Prior, the son. A further portion, a few yards north of the house occupied by Sparrow the veterinary surgeon, was sold to Smoothy on 29 July 1910. Captain, later Major, Burrows, who owned the Southend newspaper called the *Standard,* purchased it on 22 July 1938. That portion which carried on at the back of Weir Pond Road, where Smoothy had his ironworks, had been bought by Warren, now in West Street, who in turn sold out to F. Doe, Ltd., the agricultural machinery depot, who still own it. On 14 October 1947 Mrs. F. D. B. Shillan purchased the house off Burrows. The family were here until 1966, when they emigrated to Australia, where Mr. Shillan died. It was understood the property was sold to the council with some conditions attached as to its future, for Mrs. Shillan considered it to be of historical merit. The council tried to obtain permission to pull it down later after it had been boarded up, but protests from local inhabitants, the Rochford Historical Society, the Rochford Amenities Society, and others, led to a subsequent public enquiry. A position of stalemate appears to have been reached, the house still being shut up, but no further moves have been made recently. The house has now been sold privately.

It was in 1908[15] that the bay window was put in on what was in those days the front of the house. This looked out on to the Old Ship Lane, from which was the main entrance, and still today a small iron gate leads up to the house. The famous post stood outside this window, but soon after this date it was moved to a new position. W. G. Smoothy had purchased the second piece of ground off Sparrow to make sure no more building was done which blocked his view of East Street. To make absolutely certain, he had a drive constructed from this street leading up to what had been the side of the house. The post was placed some 15 feet from the side door in the centre of the carriageway. There it proved to be in the way of the old Ford family had bought, which needed a large turning circle, so it was moved left, nearer to Old Ship Lane, by Harry Smoothy. Cyril also told me that he had helped to remove the old cannon that stood upright in that lane on the opposite side, put there to prevent the carts knocking into the walls of the several cottages in the lane. He made wooden stocks to house it when the gun was placed a few yards from the post. It lay there under the shadow of a brick wall built by Mr. Shillan, who filled in the old side entrance. The cannon bears the date 1813 on its side and was recorded by Noble[16] in its former setting. The cannon now belongs to the Amenities Society and rests in the grounds of Doggett's Farm.

The house itself had a western cross-wing, probably of 16th-century origin[17] to which was added an east block in the following century, and so made the whole a T-shaped plan. There have been several modern additions at various times besides those written of, especially on the north side. At the top of the staircase there were five turned ballisters of late-17th-century workmanship.

King's Hill Cottages

These two cottages, which have had many occupants, were built some time after the house. It was thought their purpose was to house servants for the larger residence.

Father Fulcher, Snufty Brown, Sam Lancaster, Norman Smoothy, Samuel Marvin, and Mrs. Woods, were tenants listed between 1890 and 1940. In 1955 Shillan had the two converted into one for his daughter. One of the early owners of the cottage(s) was named as J. Canstatt, who had a grant of denization on 20 July 1801,[18] to make him a British citizen.

By 1813 they were in the possession of M. Lazarus and passed through many hands until they were conveyed to C. A. Shillan on 15 March 1954.[19]

Chapter Five

WATER

FROM EARLY DAYS, water has been the most essential commodity, and it was the same for Rochford. Prior to 1820, most of the water was taken from the brook for cooking, drinking, washing and cleaning, but more was required. Fortunately, there was a bed of gravel lying under much of the town, with a clay seam beneath. The gravel can be seen even today in certain parts of the stream, where it has not been sealed over or fouled with refuse. Many households had their own private supply from wells.

It was an almost impossible job to find all these, for many have fallen into disuse, some have been filled in, some lost or forgotten, and so on, but I was fortunate to discover quite a number. Perhaps I should start with the one in Ironwell Lane, well known to all the folks around. It is still there, adjoining the right-hand pillar supporting the railway arch, going down the lane from Ashingdon Road. It was a good deep well which often overflowed into the neighbouring field. As you turn into this lane, Broad Oak is on the right-hand corner with its main entrance on the Ashingdon Road. For many years this has housed the Sparrow family in retirement, yet when I called there in 1968 I was shown their well, still in good condition, save for the winding gear. It was 10 feet deep with water of a four-foot draught still in use up to 1956.

Another pump can still be seen in P. Roughton's yard, just off South Street, where soon after entry, the passage widens behind the shop. The pump had been placed on a side wall there, and the date 1828 was clearly marked with punched holes on a facing board. Across the street, but closer to Salt Bridge, was another passage often referred to as Tasker's or the Wheelwright's yard, for such it was in the 19th century, whose pump was still being used in 1955. Further down still, and over the bridge stands the *Horse and Groom* in the yard of which there remains another pump. This one, too, was well known and was much favoured by the nine or 10 householders who used to live down Watt's Lane, by the side of the public house.

An equally renowned source of water was the one in North Street which stood halfway between the *White Horse* inn and Asplin Terrace. This was always called Moll Thompson's pump, after an old lady who lived close behind it. Harry Chapman described it to me as being about five feet high, with the end for water some 18 inches from the ground. As many people came to use it, the water had to be rationed, so it was opened twice or thrice each day, with a caretaker there to check on the supply. Later it became necessary to charge for the water both as a means of repaying the wages of the watchman and to stop the too frequent use by some persons. An early custodian was Sam Tyler, who lived in a little cottage in the entry yard of the *Rose and Crown* close by. He was appointed on 30 June 1895 with a salary of 5s. 0d. per week, and instructed to charge ½d. for two pails of water, and was to open from 7.30 a.m. to 9 a.m., and 4 p.m. to 6 p.m. On 28 June 1898 T. Carter claimed 4s. 1d. wages for being keeper of the pump, and it appeared he carried on until the water began to give out. It was finally closed on 15 April 1902.

Another such water supplier was the pump close to the brook opposite the present garage of Messrs. Warren, at the bottom of West Street. On 13 August 1895[2] it had to be repaired like many of the others, when Nathaniel Kemp, the builder, did the work. H. J. Brown, nicknamed Snufty, had a general shop close by, where he housed his collection of rags, bones, and small items of furniture which he collected on his rounds with a pony and trap. He was fined on several occasions for interference with the pump, when on 19 September 1865, 24 July 1866, and again on 1 January 1867, he attempted to fence it in. The pump was finally pulled down when the new by-pass was built.

In Roche House, South Street, which for many years was a doctor's residence, but which is now part of the town's offices, there were five wells. The house had a large coach entrance and could also be approached at the back by way of Quy's Lane, East Street. Another house, opposite the Market Square, which has had many occupants, and is now the Conservative Club, had a good well, and Garrood, iron-monger, postmaster, etc., saw an eye to business, and had one dug in his garden in Back Lane, from which he sent water round the town in a large wooden barrel drawn by horse and cart. He charged ¼d. per pail in town, and ½d. outside. There were many postcards taken of this vehicle standing outside his shop in West Street. 'Little Brays House', in the lane of the same name had a good well. A. F. Stilwell had an excellent well in his steamworks at Lingfield Drive and he supplied the town with water on several occasions, such as 24 March 1898,[3] 18 January 1899[4] when he was granted 10s. for furnishing water for three days, and again on 18 April 1899[5] when the council minute book recorded it 'as the fourth day of supply at 3s. 4d. per day'. 'Chick' Robinson, painter and grainer, of East Street, had an iron cart previously used to water the roads. He had this filled from Stilwell's works, where the water was led, down a shute, across the works to the cart outside. It held 500 gallons, and Robinson[6] could time his strokes so well that 450 pumps would fill it exactly. Delivery was then made thrice daily in and around the town.

There were many more as I have said, but now to the one of greatest renown. This was the town pump in the market place, which was erected in 1820 after funds had been raised by public subscription. A plate giving this information was placed on the side of the pump. It had an iron casing approximately a foot square round it and was almost eight feet high, with an enormous weight of about 20lbs. at the end of the long curved handle. Posts were erected round, more as an ornament than a safety measure, likewise, the chains between them, since they were a bare foot above the ground.

The well was dug by Good of Maldon, who bricked it to a depth of 80 feet. Some time later the hole was bored another 100 feet to increase the flow. At first it was free, but later was put up for auction, with the bidder trying to make a bit of a living from selling water. Samuel Steward, a bootmaker from West Street, was such a person, but he employed a man to take charge. As the population increased the pump was unable to supply all needs, and economy had to be effected. This was done, as for the North Street pump by restrictions, with water only being drawn at seven o'clock in the morning, and at four in the afternoon, when payment was exacted at ¼d. a pail, or ½d a yoke. This latter was a pole, with a pail on each end, carried across the back of the neck. Benson, Johnson, and Newman were three of the keepers. The newspaper for 15 February 1896[7] commented, 'Quite a scene is witnessed in the market square every Saturday when some 60-70 children queue up for water for the following day, the charge being a farthing a pail'.

In Memoriam.

POOR OLD PUMP!

Since 1820 here I've stood,
 And yielded of my best,
And now, because I'm "not so good,"
 Folks laugh at me, and jest.

In good old ROBERT ASBEY'S time,
 I well supplied your need;
And if I rusted in my prime,
 He with *good oil* did feed.

And kept me in good order too,
 As you must surely know;
But, if you doubt my word, then you
 Had best consult FRED CROWE.—

HE knows; for many, many a time,
 He's cleaned my inner man;
And *painted* me, nor did repine,
 Deny it, if you can!

A quarter century ago
 When I was feeling queer;
The late F. SCOTT admired me so,
 He *nursed* me for a year.

He had my works all scraped and cleaned,
 And then cleared out my well;
So that the water brighter seemed,—
 But only for a spell.

For as the Towns around me grew,
 They tapped my vital spring;
And only those who *know* me, knew
 How hard I had to cling—

To keep the very life in me
 And yield the precious drink:
Alas! that I should live to see
 My poor old body *sink*?

My health, it failed, and so they sent
 To ROME, but BISHOP said—
"I'm sure 'tis of no use, ANDREW,—
"*The poor old pump is dead.*

"The Water Mains are laid you see,
 "And soon from South Benfleet
"The water will be coursing through
 "The pipes in every street.

"So let's erect a Fountain,
 "Upon the old Pump's site;
"Where naughty boys and wicked men
 "May drink and ne'er get *tight*."

　　　＊　　＊　　＊　　＊

And so, before they bury me,
 They've adorned me with this wreath;
To those who thus have honored me
 I'll *my last drops* bequeath.

　　　　　　　　　　F.W.F.

ROCHFORD.

Fig. 3　*Saturday, August 9th, 1902.*

By the kindness of Messrs. Rome and Bishop, ironmongers of the Square, I was allowed to read an old order book which gave details of the well, and said, 'it is some 50 feet from the stone kerb of the fence on south side of Connaught house and nearly 50 feet from the east corner of the saddler's shop'. This placed it in the bottom third of the Square, whereas the Market Hall had been in the top third. The well was seven to eight feet in diameter at the top, but 25 feet across at the bottom, hence termed a bell well.

Robert Asbey, the plumber, who once lived in the main part of the ironmonger's shop, and the man who so often repaired it, gave its depth as 100 feet.

It was finally demolished on Saturday, 9 August 1902. By a sad irony of fate the ironwork reposed in Smoothy's yard, Weir Pond Road for 40 years, going for the war effort in 1942.[8] The people of the town took advantage of this occasion to have a bonfire on Rutterford's meadow, now the hospital grounds, when the *Old Ship* was illuminated, special services were held in church and chapels, a bicycle carnival was held round the town, and athletic sports on Romney Marsh, now The Drive. The young children were given sandwiches, cakes and refreshments, and their elders were regaled with a meat tea, all to mark the end of the pump. Then Rochford joined with other parishes, Hockley, Rayleigh, etc., to get a piped supply from a well sunk at the top of Benfleet Hill. Each place was to pay according to its size, but only Rochford kept its promise, the others defaulted. After only a few payments, a profit of £100 was shown. Southend Waterworks put in an offer to buy the whole works and pay off the remaining debt. Rochford and others protested and in the end the case went to the House of Commons. Southend won the case, and on their undertaking to pay off the residue of £15,000 by instalments became the possessors of the well, mains, pipes, etc., together with the right to sink other wells if required.

'It was a bad business', said Francis, the printer, who represented Rochford in London. He printed a single news sheet entitled 'In Memoriam—the Poor Old Pump', in which he spoke of the loss and named the people who looked after it, like Asbey and Crowe, the plumbers, Scott, the Square's grocer, who gave money for painting, and Rome and Bishop who maintained the ironwork.

1. The Pump

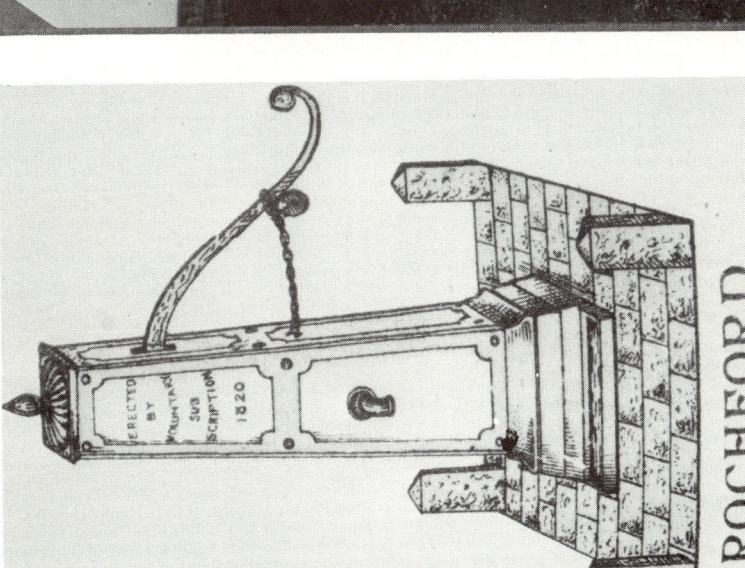

2. The Whispering Post

3. Custom House, Weir Pond Road

4. The old Cannon, dated 1813

5. The Photographer, North Street

6. The old workhouse, Southend Road

7. The Post Office, West Street

8. Market Alley

9. Rochford Hall, north side

10. The old barn, Hall Road

11. Old Post Office, 1880

12. Rochford Market

13. The *Rose and Crown*

14. Hartley's the Saddler, founded 1777

Chapter Six

AGRICULTURE

THE AREA OF ROCHFORD was given by the Tithe Commutation map of 1840 as 1,855 acres 3 roods 10 poles[1] of which 38 acres 2 roods 5 poles were then road and waste. Benton said the soil was good generally, especially where the east and central districts were close to the town[2] with the soil nearer Canewdon stronger. To the west, nearer to Eastwood he declared its character to change to a stiff and adhesive consistency, whilst on the Hawkwell border it was heavy and often strong. Coller[3] said the Rochford Hundred possessed some of the finest soil in the kingdom, whilst Arthur Young in 1813[4] said that the soil of Rochford Hall, where Wright farmed was 'mellow, friable, reddish loam up to two feet thick and adjoined a vein of darker hue, keeping its colour well, even when dry'. Chamberlayne[5] said the soil in some places was so rich that after three years of growing saffron, good barley could be raised for 20 years without dunging. The rent was then between 20s. and 21s. an acre; tithes were 5s. 8d. great and small, and the poor rate was 7s. 6d. Young further stated that Wright never worked two crops of white corn in succession. The covenants of the lease under which Rochford Hall was held prescribed: (1) fallow; (2) oats or barley; (3) clover; (4) wheat; (5) oats or barley. Peas and beans were seldom mentioned, but the use of a heavy roller was advocated to combat the depradations of wireworm. Young said that the land round Rochford was often ploughed seven to eight times for cereal crops, and that Wood, who managed the Hall farm after Wright died, advocated deep ploughing. The cost of ploughing he gave as 10s. 6d. per acre. Wright used to dibble his wheat in, holding it to be the right practice, except for the expense, since it cost double the normal per acre. He especially liked American Red seed, which yielded well he proclaimed.

We know that little care was taken early in the practice of good husbandry, and crop rotation, and that mildew was rife. In 1783 one man in Rochford had only three bushels of cereal for the acre, and this not good even for fowls. Wright again recommended American white wheat to be cut green, 'for if it be brittle it do lose ears': he expected five quarters in a good year of wheat. Towards the end of 1800 progress in the cultivation of land was slow, Benton stated[6] and weedy stubble was fired by farmers, including Cannon Barrington. He had the lease of Doggett's farm from 1777 to 1784, and his son, John, from 1802 to 1828. Many farmers, including the lessee of Rochford Hall, oversowed with wheat, which practice Benton said,[7] wasted the seed and diminished the crop. They also trod the ground with horses, bullocks and sheep as another remedy against wireworm and prescribed hunting on the land as of great benefit. Few gave thought to laying down land to grass and sweepings were deemed adequate to sow, whilst for manure the residue that had been used for potash-making was considered sufficient; farm dung was too frequently turned, but chalk was much used. Young[8] indicated a Hockley farmer called Hicks who had used 1,000 tons of chalk on 11 acres of land.

The Lincoln breed of sheep were generally kept before crosses and Southdowns were introduced, and Berkshire hogs were largely bred and folded on clover. The cattle that were maintained were all run together, few sheds existed,

Agriculture　　　　　　　　　　　　　　　　　　　　35

and little extra feeding was undertaken. A few farmers were evidently more far-sighted, for Young in about 1790 described a threshing machine[9] used by Dr. Asplin of Little Wakering Hall, worked by only one horse, driven by a girl. which beat three quarters of wheat in a day, but cost 60 guineas. In 1882 it was converted to a chaff cutter.

Superstition was prevalent; barberry bushes were believed to induce mildew in wheat, other farmers never ploughed in snow, holding that it produced may-weed; one never sowed oats on Ash Wednesday for fear of *bottling* them, whilst another sowed cole seed at night to check the fly.[10] Spring sowing of corn and other crops was little practised. A great change took place in agriculture from the middle of the 19th century. By that date steam ploughing had been introduced with two huge machines which stood on each side of a field and used a steel hawser attached to a plough. By this means, four, sometimes six, furrows could be worked at once, or a large cultivator could be used so the soil could be worked deeper than by horse and man. At Great Doggett's farm there was an old horse gin which was still there in 1969. From the height of the shed in which it was installed I believe ponies or bullocks were used to power it. A series of belts and pulleys converted it for various purposes.

Food riots occurred in various parts of England in the late 18th century and beyond, In 1772,[11] one such occurred in Rochford (see Police). In a Commissioners' report for 1836[12] a statement was made that one reason for the absence of able-bodied paupers was the good crop of the previous harvest. It went on to say that wheat was rotting in Rochford Hundred and other parts for want of hands to reap it, and that, at a guinea and 24s. an acre. So there were good times as well as bad, and Rochford had its share of both. It was forthcoming with the production and use of machines, for

John Offord sold Lodge field, part of Coombes farm (which he bought in 1867) to Arthur Carey for his steam plough works. This was about 1870[13] when Carey's name is first recorded as an engineer. The site today is covered with houses, and called Lingfield Drive. The firm of F. W. Smoothy began in East Street to the side of the *New Ship* inn before 1882[14] but after a few years it moved to Weir Pond Road and continued to 1945.

Wages have always been low in the industry, and up to the end of the 19th century, farm wages were often no more than £1 per week, although there was often a free cottage included as a perk. Free of rent it might have been, but it was tied to the possessor being at work on the farm. Farms for rent were then costing 20s. to 35s. an acre, with the staffing ratio of one man and two horses to 40 acres of arable land considered sufficient.

Chapter Seven

THE TWO FIRES

IN THE DAYS when most entertainment was either homemade or consisted of a night out at the inn, at least by the men folk, any excuse was used to have a bonfire as a spectacle. One such was made to commemorate the end of the town pump, the demise of which I have recorded in a separate chapter. The *Southend Standard* reported the happening in the paper dated 15 August 1902.[1] My chapter here is of two fires that were of an entirely different character.

The first fire was accidental, but it did much harm, for on 9 July 1884 it broke out in Robert Asbey's shop in the Square. He was a plumber, selling oil and paint as well. His shop, that of William Stocks the butcher, next door, F. Scott the grocer, next to him, and the *Star* inn beyond, were all badly damaged. This last was an off-licence in the corner of the Square, always a newspaper shop after that. Two of the four cottages in the Alley were also badly damaged. The first, next to the *Star* collapsed almost immediately, the second had to be pulled down days afterwards. The police station on North Street, now the post office, also suffered losses to its sheds at the back, as did some stables next to it. Rome and Bishop's, the other side of Asbey, had damage, too. The total was estimated at £10,000, which was quite a sum in those days.

When the fire was first seen, a man standing near the *King's Head* opposite, grabbed a horse tethered nearby and rode to Southend for the fire brigade. This, when it came, stationed itself a little way down West Street, so one hose could reach the flames and the other could go into the brook at the bottom of West Street. So far so good; but, unfortunately, the summer had been a dry one and so was the brook, for after only a few minutes the pump stopped working as the pipes were unable to suck up any water. So the fire raged on unchecked save for the efforts made by onlookers who pulled articles, especially furniture, out of the way. By the time it subsided the damage had occurred. When all was cleared up, F. Scott rented a shop just a few yards away from his former business at the corner of the market, next to Connaught House. Mann, who had been Scott's assistant, then took over, buying the next shop down West Street on the north side, which Hall once used.

The second fire was indeed different for it was deliberate, and was begun to celebrate the relief of Mafeking. On the 17 May 1900, this town in South Africa was relieved. So, too, was Rochford . . . of much feeling, much wood and other combustible material. The citizens here decided to show their pleasure with a bonfire. Where else to hold it but the Square, scene of so many events and happenings? Let me say at once it was no organised affair, far from it.

It began simply enough, but rapidly got out of hand. At first paper, a few boxes, palings and other rubbish was used, but then other materials appeared. Mr. McBryer, whose saddler's shop was down the bottom of West Street, remembered an old cart stuck in the hedge, near Carey's Cottages on Stambridge Road. With a little help it was hauled out and heaved on the fire. By this time at least two others had been broken up and thrown on, one of which was the special cart with a cranked axle to lower it to the ground in order to lift the huge tubs of fat used in candle-making on more easily. Henry Mann's cart, which he used to deliver groceries, followed in its turn, and other articles of wood that could be found. As if this was not enough, a doctor living nearby in Roche House, South Street, who had heard the commotion, came from his house and ran to the Square, where he promptly gave 2s. 6d. to a bystander to fetch a couple of barrels of tar from the gasworks in East Street. This last item was a little too much for the police, and Inspector Chase at the station was informed. He came hurrying out and was just in time to see the cart with the barrels on, coming down Old Ship Lane. He attempted to prevent its progress by pushing at it from the front, but other people assisted those on the cart and he was knocked down. Fortunately for him, for the weight was considerable, the wheels passed on either side of him. He sought assistance from two magistrates who were onlookers, but they advised him to turn a blind eye on this occasion.

By now the noise of the fire and from the crowd, had drawn many people to the scene: some carried material to burn, others were waving flags. This added to the excitement and the danger, for several of these caught fire so were waved about to try to extinguish them. Those close at hand suffered damage to clothes and person, which made many realise the extent of the conflagration. The tar by then was hot, so melted, and burning, it began to trickle down the Square, which has always had a slope into West Street, where the gradient increases. There it blocked the gulleys and began to run over on to the path where it stuck to the feet of people passing. Attempts were then made to put out the flames, but so great had the fire become that little could be done for some time. Sand, earth, and finally water succeeded in checking the outbreak. So ended rather sadly what had begun as a happy occasion.

Chapter Eight

RELIGION

Rochford Church

THIS IS A RED BRICK structure standing very close to the Hall, from whose brickyards it was said to have obtained its supply. It is dedicated to St. Andrew and, Benton said, consisted of a nave, north and south aisles, a south porch and a high embattled tower with three bells.[1] Muilman[2] said the aisles, chancel and north chapel were leaded, and the remainder tiled. The tower is a fine example of the use of Essex bricks, which are interspersed with Reigate stone to form a diaper pattern in black, for there was no stone hereabouts to use. No date has been given by Benton, who declared the church's structure to belong to the Decorated period, with many portions containing remains of 14th-century work, though Thomas Boteler, Earl of Ormond, who died in 1515, probably rebuilt it. Others suggest Lord Rich had a hand in it, especially as regards the steeple, but since Boteler's arms were on it, this seems to give him first choice. Moul[3] gives the date as in the reign of Henry VII. Benton stated that the sacristy was added in that reign, which blocked up one of the decorated windows on the north. This might have been a chapel, he indicated.[4] It had a hagioscope which pierced the wall towards the high altar. The east window was of the Perpendicular period, with five lights, the head being filled with mullioned tracery. The west doorway had moulded jambs, a four-centred porch

Religion

with a label, above which a sunken panel had a stone shield. It was here that the arms of Ormond were displayed.

In the north aisle there was a tomb nearly 600 years old with a Latin inscription which translated reads, 'Pray for the soul of Anne Snokehill, daughter of John Filol of Landermere who lieth here; God have mercy and compassion on her soul, who died St. Valentine's day in the year of Jesus Christ 1386'. In the middle of the church was a grave to Maria Dilcock, who died 13 April 1514. Muilman records the body of Stephen Jackson of Great Doggetts, who died in 1706,[5] as being close to the east window, and added that in the churchyard were tombs of Richard Knight recording his death on 9 June 1702, and to John Fortescue, who died 18 August 1710, aged 63 years.

The stained glass windows in the south were a present from Mrs. Gardiner, widow of Rev. William Gardiner, who was inducted in 1837. He died in 1861 and one of the two windows depicted his sufferings, for his epitaph mentioned 14 years of pain. On the north-east a window was placed in memory of Augusta, wife of William Gregson, solicitor here from 1830, who died 20 January 1852. The tower once had four bells, but Sir William Stafford appropriated three of them to repair the walls at Foulness.[6] The remaining one was found to be cracked in 1873.

The bell foundry at Whitechapel East submitted a bill for £153 for refitting three new bells on 27 November 1873. Mrs. Tawke of 'The Lawn' was the instigator in the fundraising appeal, and Benton has it that Mears and Stainbank of London cast them.[8] It was a standing reproach to the chief town of the Hundred that it never got a peal of bells, he said.

The whole church has had many restorations, both large and small. Weld, the bricklayer, did much work here, and

Elizabeth Allen did sewing and needlework repairs to the interior fabrics. Her bill was dated 19 March 1778. On 6 September William Hitchcock the carpenter's bill was for £112, whilst on 28 March 1780 a new altar-piece cost nearly £9. In 1827 a gallery was added, and the high pews were removed.[9] Between 1830 and 1842 running repairs were effected to all parts by Allen, the carpenter, by Freeman, Codlin and Clark for ironwork, and Burgess for glazing. In 1835 some 12,500 bricks were bought from T. Stebbings at 34s. a thousand. Then in 1862[10] major works were completed with William Slater, a London architect in charge, at a cost of £2,000. On 15 August 1872 the Rev. Cotton wrote to the Lord Bishop of Rochester about proposed changes to the choir-stalls by alteration of the chancel.[11] It was while this was being done that a scratching was noticed on the jamb of a south-west window of the chancel; the name Samuel Purkas 1642 was made out.[12] His Lordship replied on 20 August that year and issued a decree for the work. A plan was then made to accomplish this.[13] It appears also that the churchyard had become full, for the lord of the manor was asked to give a small piece of land to increase the size. This apparently was granted, since in 1870 an addition to the ground was consecrated.[14] On 5 April 1896 Rev. Cotton sold some glebe land, and with the proceeds bought half an acre of land bordering the churchyard, which he gave to the church.[15] This was blessed in 1898.[16] Once more, in 1938, extensive repairs, costing over £1,000, were carried out, and two cottages were then built at the rectory from the remains of the old stable.

The rectory had always been appended to the manor, and Newcourt affirmed that the earliest date recorded of the patronage was 1279, adding that when John de Rochford was patron, there was a vicarage here, which was dissolved

Religion 43

shortly afterwards, but that a rectory was instituted
c. 1321.[17] Muilman put the date as early as 1219. The list
that follows gives some of the vicars with their advowsen.

    John Berryman, who died in 1572.[18]

Robert, Earl of Warwick inducted—
    William Fenner in 1629, died 1639;
    Edward Calamy, 9 November 1637, resigned 1639;[19]
gave living to—
    Nicholas Beard, A.M. 1639;
inducted—
    Daniel Weld, 19 March 1655, who died in 1670.

Charles, Earl of Warwick to—
    John Benson in 1670–78
    William Benson, his brother, who died in 1680.

Charles, Earl of Warwick to—
    James Symonds, A.M., 1680, who resigned in 1691.

Henry St. John gave living to—
    John Lister, who died in 1737.

Richard, Earl Tylney to—
    Dr. Wm. Henry Thomlinson, 1735–75.[20]

John, Earl Tylney admitted—
    R. Berkeley, 11 April 1778–1814;
    Andrew Windsor, 1814–April 1837, aged 73;
    William Gardiner, 1837–42, who died 9 Sept. 1861, aged 57.

Wm. Richard, Earl of Mornington inducted—
    Benjamin Cotton, M.A.

From the records of St. Mary the Virgin church, Great Warley, Essex, in the baptismal register of 1539 is the following: 'Cristyninges 1703, John, ye bastard son of Dorothy Scot (who she fathered upon John Johnston of Rochford town) was baptized upon ye 23 day of October'.

The Rev. Wise, vicar of Nevendon and curate here was a well-known figure in the district, very active in promoting its welfare. He made the 1803 Inventory,[21] after the invasion scare following Napoleon's threats to England. His concern about the market has been expressed in that chapter. He persuaded Sir James Tylney Long to enlarge the churchyard in 1791.[22] He suggested, to save expense that the consecration be deferred until the Bishop of London made his proposed visit the following year. He also wrote to the bailiff of the Manor Court about beating the bounds in a letter dated 30 January 1804, wherein he said it was some 17 or 18 years since it had been done, when the cost was shared by the lord of the manor, who gave two-thirds of the cost, and Rev. Berkeley the remainder. Wise was also an acting magistrate for the district. He was born in 1756 and died on 12 March 1814, having served Rochford for 32 years as assistant priest.

Other Denominations

In a letter from the Rochford rectory dated 6 July 1829[23] written by W. W. Robinson, it stated that besides the church there was a Methodist chapel, an Independent, and a Wesleyan place of worship. The letter was addressed to G. Parker, Esq., Springfield Place, Chelmsford.

(a) The Presbyterians

They were here very early, for a return made to the Registrar General in 1699 recorded the house of Henry Vassall as

Religion 45

their chapel. The preacher's name was also given as Thomas Scalbott, but no more was found of this faith.

(b) The Congregationals
In Lord Rich's time the Independents began to flourish here under the protection of the Hall, where a chapel was built for their worship in 1581, since largely destroyed. Afterwards they were said to have met in a building in Weir Pond Road, close to where it meets East Street. True enough there was a rounded door in an old part of the works of F. Doe, but no other traces of religious service. They then moved to a small building in North Street where a vestry was built in 1690. The first preacher named as William Condor in 1716 was not ordained, but from 1734 they had a regular preacher. Before that a supply of preachers had come from the religious academy of Dr. Doddridge of Northampton. On 27 May 1841 Nicholas Bowles, a victualler, probably of the *Old Ship* nearby, sold some land to William Wallman, who let it to the congregation. Rev. Ebenezer Temple, born 19 March 1807, who came to Rochford on 20 March 1836, is credited with enlarging the building. Many people told me he had the middle portion of the church added, but an architect who recently examined the two sets of brickwork was of the opinion that the front portion near the street was the new addition. In the central portion many bricks had initials of people carved in to signify their help in defraying the cost of £500. So perhaps that was where the theory took shape. Eli Beckwith, the schoolmaster, and George Raymond, the tailor, have their names in full, but for others, the initials only, present a problem. Thus J.W. could be John Wiseman, the oyster merchant, W.T. perhaps William Topsfield, H.W. maybe Henry Wood, the rate collector, G.C. possibly George Carter, a builder, and R.B.

the letters of Robert Bright, innkeeper. Certainly W. P. Kernot's name or initials were not found, though he gave a considerable sum towards its cost. Temple, who had written the *Christians' Daily Treasury* in 1835, just before coming here, compiled a second volume in 1836. After his death in 1841, his wife and friends published his collected sermons. Perhaps the most famous minister here was Rev. Thomas Hayward, who came in August after Temple died. He served the flock here for over 40 years and received a subscription in August 1877 so well was he revered. By the time he had died on 2 April 1888 he had seen, devised and helped in many alterations including a new gallery in 1866 costing £47. Just after his death the building was re-seated at a cost of £80. It was in 1907 that the Independents joined with the Essex Congregationals, thereafter taking this name. They had a very well known choir in the early 19th century when Raymond, the tailor, conducted, John Allen played the cello, and his son, William, the viola. The old Manse in South Street, next but one to the ironmongers, was given as a dwelling house for the priest by the said William Wallman, farmer of Southchurch Wick, in 1750. Previously it had been occupied by William Parkin, a glazier up to 1741. The house was purchased finally by Rochford Council after protracted discussion, but was badly damaged by fire about ten past three on the afternoon of 5 September 1968, but it was not pulled down until January 1971. Today it houses part of the Council's officials after rebuilding.

(c) The Wesleyans
These people were here before 1825,[24] using a small house[25] at the end of Market Alley as it turns into the Square. Then another building in North Street was used which was held on lease, dated 27 April 1841, but it was not solemnised for

Religion 47

marriages until 1852. J. Whybrew, a local preacher, who now lives in Grested Court, East Street, told me in 1968 when I called to see him, that the chapel had been converted into three cottages, and on stripping the walls of the one he was in, the bill of authorisation was found. Mr. Whybrew was unable to recall the exact date, but estimated it as about 1929. It was William Bishop, the draper, who had undertaken the reconversion. The present building lies some 50-60 yards further down North Street, but still on the same side, and was built in 1880 after John George Baxter of Southend made a handsome grant towards the total cost of £800. A Sunday school was built on the side in 1897 on the site of a copse which George Wood, solicitor, had purchased from Barnabas Townsend, the potash maker.

(d) The Baptists

There was a Baptist chapel built on the east side of South Street, just north of the present police station. The house is one of those that stand out from the line of other buildings. It was only the front room of a house, some 15 feet square, so there was only a small following. It was pulled down in 1890 and was replaced by the present building very appropriately called 'Zion Villa'. Nathan Kemp, a builder, used materials he had obtained when he knocked down Little Stambridge church in 1891. He used a vestry door as part of the front window on to South Street. The chapel is listed in 1872[26] and is marked on the Ordnance Survey map of 1873. The full name of the sect was the Society of Strict Communion Baptists.

(e) The Peculiar People

James Banyard was born on 31 January 1800 to the wife of a ploughman of Rochford Hall. In early years he was a scoffer at religion as well as a poacher and almost a ne'er-do-well, but he changed profoundly in his later years. He first became a shoemaker and then turned to religion on hearing visiting preachers. He joined the Methodists, but withdrew because of their opposition to his views on simplicity. He then came under the influence of William Bridges, a London hat-block maker, who visited Rochford in 1838 to see his sister. Bridges' opinions had been established by hearing the views of Atkins, a minister from the established church of the Isle of Man, who condemned the formalism of the church and service.

Banyard had already begun to set up a small circle of his own by having meetings in his cottage at the lower end of West Street on the south side, but had to find fresh premises when his landlord made objections since the windows of the small house had been broken by the stones of jeering mobs. So he moved to a house in the lane close to the Union gates, where he continued preaching to a score of people. However, after two years here, the growth in the numbers made conditions cramped, and a larger house in Barrack Lane, almost opposite, was hired. He was allowed to knock out the walls to make a chapel which could then hold nearly a hundred people. Yet still the number of his converts grew so that he had to search for larger premises.

Finally he married Judith Knapping, and with her money he was able to buy a building in North Street in 1850.[27] Some sources indicated that new premises were constructed, but I was given information[28] that it was a building used by the Wesleyans beforehand. This was sold on Thursday, 30 June 1878, after having been let for some time to Samuel Harrad of Hawkwell. This is a name that occurred frequently in reports of the sect, as did that of Banyard's wife, Knapping. Their faith in Divine healing was based on the Epistle to St. James, and they held great store in both prayer and annointing; so much so that they opposed medical aid as an inquest on Joshua James Robinson on 10 May 1900[29] showed. He was a carpenter, aged 56, who would not have a doctor called in as he was of the faith, but insisted on being annointed by William Heddle, an elder from Southend.

The men wore bowler hats, whilst the women had large bonnets. Meetings were held four times on Sunday, at 6 a.m. for prayer, at 10.30 a.m. for praise and testimony, 2.30 p.m. for prayers again, and at 6.30 p.m. for preaching; besides which they had gatherings on Tuesday and Thursday evenings. In 1852 when the group was well established they concluded to have four bishops, and chose Banyard, Harrad, David Handley, and John Thorogood. Their cause spread to surrounding places, especially Great Wakering and Maldon, where strong branches were formed. During their time they were called various names, such as Banyardites, Newlights, and even Ranters, but settled for the name United Brethren.

In 1855 Banyard was deposed, for he had called in a doctor to attend his son (not his daughter as is often given). This fact caused a split in the ranks which also led to a loss of members. Banyard himself died soon after on 31 October 1863, and was buried by the south wall of Rochford church. After this, the name Peculiar was adopted by the Maldon branch.

Many miracles were claimed by the order, the most important being a case of reclaimed sight, of recovery from a severe illness, and others of less importance, such as lockjaw; but the elders tried to play these down. W. Wood, who lived at the corner of Old Ship Lane and East Street, a carpenter and wheelwright, and an early maker of penny-farthing bicycles, was a later leader from 1872 to 1914, whilst John Anderson, a thatcher from South Street, was a more recent local preacher.

Soon after 1910, when several members had suffered prosecution following their refusal to call in medical assistance, which in one case resulted in a child's death, another split came, and a Liberty branch was formed, one of whose tenets was to allow a doctor's help in cases of child illnesses. In 1904 Bishop Heddle, one of the elders, advanced money to build a chapel in Townfield Road. This has had a change of name, and is today called Rocheway. The sect then joined up with the Evangelicals. Heddle gave money towards the building of two houses next to the building, which were then called 'The Laurels', but now have the numbers 18 and twenty. They were for a caretaker and a follower of the denomination.

Chapter Nine

THE BANKS

THERE WAS AN early bank in Rochford just before 1800, but nothing has been found about it. However, in the early part of 1826 one began here called the Rochford and Billericay bank.[1] The partners were Messrs. M. B. and J. W. Harvey. We have a saying today 'as safe as the Bank of England', but this definitely was not the case with the town's early banks, for this one soon folded up. It was then taken up by William and George Jackson, the first of whom had the early printing press here. Regrettably, this bank, too, failed. There seems some confusion about the early banks, for Glyn Mills, of London, who seem to have been part sponsors for the firm gave me J. and W. Mew as the first bankers, which view Glennie[2] took in his book called *Our Town*, who then said Jackson followed.

After the attempt by the Jacksons, various influential people approached James Giles, manager of the former banks, to start a new concern. Rankin, the miller, T. S. Scratton, of the Priory, Kernot, the druggist, were among the guarantors. He agreed, and set up an establishment on the south side of West Street in a house later called 'Danehurst', which afterwards became the shop of Ling, the carpenter. Giles retired in 1853 when Sparrow, Tufnell and Co. from Chelmsford took it over in June of that year. Edward Trotter Jackson, who had married Mary Ann Giles, was appointed in his father-in-law's place, for just after retiring James died, aged sixty-eight. Soon after the new bank had been built in 1866, on the site of the old *Vernon's Head*, Mary passed away, but her husband carried on until 1884. He was the father of Edward 'Teddie' Jackson, whose pack of beagles was a well-known sight and sound in and around Rochford. This began in 1869, and the hounds were kept in Back Lane at first, but later they moved to Smith and Chamberlain's farm in Greensward Lane, Hockley. Teddie was born at 'Gothic Cottage', Stroud Green. It was believed this was rebuilt as part of the new residence for Evan's farm. Later father and son moved to 'The Lavenders', West Street, for a short period, but ended up at Sydenham House, South Street. Teddie published a book on the *Foot Beagles of Essex*. A hunting horn used by him was bequeathed to the museum at Prettlewell Priory. It was inscribed E.J. 1869-71, which Benton[3] said he received in 1877, together with a purse of money.

It was not until 1896 that the name of Barclay and Co., Ltd., was established here. Early directories gave A. K. Bevan as manager, but this should have been Alfred Keely Kevan, who was in charge until 1904. After this, Rochford was subjugated to Southend until 1914, when F. J. Diaper came. It had opened daily, but then changed to a thrice-weekly service on Tuesday, Thursday and Saturday. In February 1917 it became known as Barclay's Bank Ltd., with H. J. Taylor conducting the business, then when he left in 1922 it became a full branch again, but under a Southend manager. A. E. Prior was manager from 1925-31, then again it had full separate status under F. A. Roger in 1947. H. W. Humphries had a long stay until 1958, when followed a quick succession of managers.

There was a small bank, using various names, but chiefly called the Westminster Banking Company, whose premises were in the Market Square opposite the present bank of Barclay. It only opened on market day, Thursday, from 10.30 a.m. to 3.30 p.m., with staff from a main branch at Southend, who took the money back at the end of the day. It was where is today the small window of the saddler's shop, on the left when entering the premises. It began about 1887 and continued until 1940. A few years later the present Westminster Bank opened in South Street on 1 March 1954. This bank has now returned to the Square and adjoins Connaught House, on the site of a house called 'Fernside' (see Chapter 2). It will face a new road, proposed to run northwards at the rear of the properties in North Street.

Chapter Ten

THE SCHOOLS

THERE WAS A SCHOOL in Rochford as early as 1628, for in that year a Mr. Love was named as master with Etham Glasscock, who became a tailor at Pritwell [early spelling] as a pupil before he went on to Maldon, and then to Sydney Sussex College. In Pigot's first directory of 1823/4 H. H. Fragniere was shown, but he could well have been here before that, since an earlier reference was in the 1803 Invasion returns, a gap of 20 years. His school, Rochford Academy, was for boarders, and a pupil here was James Clark, whose mother, Hannah, lived at North Shoebury Hall. A copy of the bill for his board and lodgings for 1829 is shown (4a). Dr. Asplin[1] wrote of treating the schoolmaster after he had been thrown out of his gig. The school was at the house called 'The Lavenders',[2] near the end of West Street on the north side. In his time it was a large L-shaped building with plenty of barns and outhouses to it. These were later taken down and formed Lavender Square. Again in the 1960s a large piece was taken off the house, so today it is but one-third or less of its former size.

Eli Beckwith, 1790-1841, was at the early British school in the year 1823-39.[3] He doubled up in the trades of bookbinder and thatcher, and had a house in Weir Pond Road. The school was in the grounds of the present Congregational church in North Street, where Eli was assisted by his two sons, both of whom died early, and from then on by his

The Schools

daughter, Ann. Early pupils paid 1d. per week and had to provide their own slates and pencils. Tom Butcher and his daughter were next in charge, but in 1840 a new school was built on land given by the Tabor family of Braintree, which had been accepted by the resident minister, Rev. T. Hayward. No deed was found of this gift, so in 1907 Harry Chapman drew up plans for its registration. Noble wrote[4] that the infant school had a tablet on its outer wall saying, 'the eavesdrop to the extent of nine inches belongs to this building, 1839'. After a long search I found this still inserted on the outside wall of the *Old Ship*.

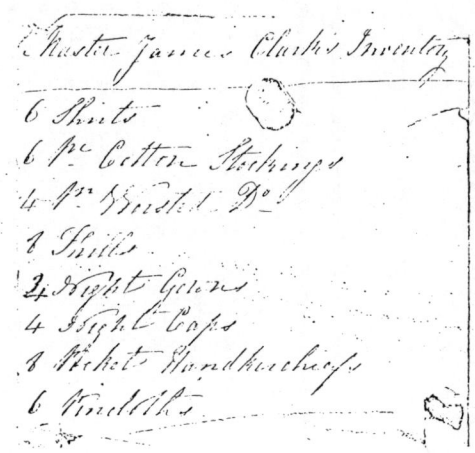

Fig. 4a

A report on schools in Essex for 1808[5] gave four schools in the town, with one Sunday school, and continued by saying one day school had about 50 pupils who partly supported it (so it was probably the British school) with the remainder defrayed by the parishioners. The three other schools were given as having about 90 pupils between them, whilst the Sunday school had 40 children supported by voluntary contributions of half from the vicar, Rev. Berkeley, a quarter by the curate, Rev. J. Wise, and the rest by the people. Mrs. Anne Allen's school was one of the three listed, for hers was a boarding school in what was

Rochford Academy.

Mrs Clark Dr.

To H. H. Fragnier

1828		£	s	d
Xmas. To the Board & Tuition of Master Clark				
from Midst to Xmas		10	10	0
To Writing £1.1 — Mendg. 2/6		1	3	6
To Exercising			1	6
To Medicent				6
To Shoecleaning			2	0
To Pens & Ink			2	6
To 2 Copy Books			2	6
To 2 Murray's Abridgmt.			2	2
To a Bible			6	1
To 2 Marvel Shelly Books			3	2
To Do. of the Sacred				3
To a Set of Cart. of Paper				2
To 22 Weeks Pocket Money @ 2			3	8
Fr. Schoolmaster as pr of B		19	0
To a Tailor as pr of C		4	1
		13	**16**	**10**

The School will re-open on the 19th of Jan 1829.

Fig. 4b Rochford Academy : Bill of 1828

King's Hill, Rochford, Essex.

Miss RAYNHAM receives a limited number of Pupils to Board and Educate upon the following terms:—

		£	s	d
Boarders,	per quarter ...	5	15	0
Weekly ditto	,, ...	4	10	0
Day ditto,	,, ...	2	15	0
Music,	,, ...	1	1	0
French,	,, ...	0	10	6
Laundress	,, ...	0	10	6
Day Scholars,	,, ...	1	1	0
Ditto, under Eight	,, ...	0	15	0
Ditto, under Six	,, ...	0	10	6

QUARTER COMMENCING AT TIME OF ENTRANCE.

A Quarter's notice respectfully requested previous to the removal of a Pupil.

KNIFE AND FORK, TOWELS ETC., WILL BE RETURNED.

Fig. 4c King's Hill School Prospectus 1888

The Schools

later called Sydenham House in South Street, where it continued up to 1845.[6] Tom Richardson was another who had a private school, and Peter Pond was named as headmaster of the Free school in 1820 with a salary of £10 per quarter. Some confusion existed over the naming of these schools since another document of 1812[7] spoke of the National School, so perhaps the word Free was synonymous with National.

In 1837 a school board was set up and a National school built on the end of West Street, just before it turns into the main road with a school house on that very end. John Popplewell was its first headmaster, but he found the house not quite finished, so he rented a place on Dale Road, the name given then to the present Ashingdon Road. This old thatched cottage was still on the 1890 map, listed as 'The Nursery'. His salary was £46 per annum for himself and his wife, Phoebe, and on it they reared a family of twelve.

The old school still stands, but is now called the Church Institute, and strangely enough it serves as a nursery school today. A census taken soon after the school was opened found there were 135 pupiles present, from Hawkwell, Eastwood, Sutton, and Rochford.[8] The school had two rooms, one each for boys and girls, of approximately 23 feet by 22 feet, separated by framed partitions, whilst a small entrance porch was built on as an extra. In 1840/41 attendance reached 212, so rebuilding was needed, but it was delayed until 1855/6, for the National Society, despite all appeals made to it, would only donate £12 towards an estimate of £115. It was only then that gas was installed. It had some peculiar rules, such as that for payment, for the 1d. a day had to be made in advance, no child under six to be admitted, no-one unless vaccinated, every third child in a family to be allowed in free, but a fine of ½d.

was imposed for an excuse for absence that was thought to be invalid. A two-day bazaar was held twice annually, when articles made by the children were sold. These were mostly needlework, such as aprons, collars, handkerchiefs, shirts with frills, which sold for 1s. 6d., and nightcaps for 4d. The proceeds went toward the costs of the school, but donations, annual subscriptions, and the odd grant were sought. All these proved insufficient, for in 1870 the school was £120 in debt. When John died in 1873, his wife went to live at 'Eastwood Villa,' one of a pair of houses on Southend Road, now graced with the number thirty. This she opened as a day school, mainly for shopkeepers' children, whom she charged 6d. weekly. Meanwhile Ancel Culling had arrived as head of the National School and remained until 1888.

Sydenham House had since re-opened as a boarding school, run by George Foster, who came from Sydenham, Kent, hence the name. This was in 1858[9] and the school remained here until after 1873, when Miss S. Raynham took it over. She had already started a school for young ladies, using part of King's Hill for boarders and day pupils at terms shown on the prospectus. (See 4c)

There were other boarding and day schools in the town: for example, in 1832, besides Beckwith, Allen, Fragniere, Griffin, and Richardson, five other schoolmistresses were named as Mrs. Brady, Mrs. Lamprell, Miss Osborn, Miss Thorpe, and Miss Passey, together with Rev. Fawcett, and all gave lessons. The last-named had disappeared by 1835, but the other four remained in directories up to 1845, when they were joined by the Misses Harriet and Henrietta May. Fortunately, W. Francis went to this school for a short period and gave the location as next to the *Golden Lion* in North Street. He then joined T. Richardson's school

The Schools

which was in East Street, opposite the *New Ship*. His school remained listed up to 1859[10] but in 1862[11] John Mills' name appeared as taking over from Richardson. Francis had meanwhile gone to 'the Church school when Mr. Richardson died, then back to Mr. Mills' school'. The 1874 directory records Mrs. Hannah Ventris, to whom another member of the Francis family went in his very early boyhood for he said that he learned his alphabet and a few words from her. From his description this must have been down West Street, on the north side, where it carried on as a day school. The list grows sparser after this, with only Mrs. Popplewell, Miss Raynham, and A. Culling's names given in the next three directories of 1878, 1882, and 1886. In 1890 T. Histed's name takes the place of A. Culling as head teacher. Another report on schools in Essex for 1870[12] gave the population of Rochford as 1,500, and the places in schools as two hundred.

By now the Rochford primary school was built on the Ashingdon Road a few yards from the old National school. A stone plaque with the date 1877 was placed on the walls in the centre of a middle playground for the school was constructed like a letter E, with classrooms in each wing, boys one end, girls the other, separated by a long corridor which joined the two. It cost £4,000, and was meant to hold 400 children. In 1896 it was enlarged to take in more infants and again in 1900 when, in building on new classrooms and a head teacher's room and staff room, the playground was filled in so the plaque can only be seen from inside. A headmaster's house was built between the old and new schools at the same time. Many alterations were carried out in the next few years, and a very interesting letter was found at the Record Office on this subject dated 10 September 1878[13]. Charles Pertwee, architect of Chelmsford wrote to

George Wood, solicitor here, asking him to arrange terms for repair with Allen, the carpenter, 'who, I have no doubt, will honestly carry out what he undertakes to do'.

Of equal curiosity was the school of Rev. Bryers, vicar of Ashingdon from 1912 to 1923,[14] which was in two parts. One for the older pupils, was contained at the vicarage, the other for younger boys, who were taught in the mornings, at 'Little Brays'. In this house in Bray's Lane, Rochford, lived three Church of England nuns. There was Sister Mary, who taught English and mathematics; Sister Margaret, whose subjects were history and geography; and Sister Faith, who instructed some of the girl pupils who boarded with them in needlework. When Prince Chula of Siam (now Thailand) came to the school at the vicarage he wrote that there were 12 boarders.[15] Nine had come from Harrow school for intensive coaching before proceeding to Cambridge. In his book, Chula said his cousin, Prince Chumbhot, was there the year before him. The school ran from 1916 to 1939 when all three sisters retired to live at 28 Oak Road. Besides the house, the sisters used two railway carriages they had bought and installed in the grounds. These were still in place when I called in 1967 to see the owner, Mrs. Robertson, wife of the chemist from West Street. I saw a small window in the bathroom, all that remained of a small chapel for morning worship. A pulpit also had been in the room when Mrs. Robertson had first come.

Another small school of much later date was one called 'The Priors', running from 1940 to 1951, being a branch of a similar school in Southend, both under the supervision of Miss E. C. Coombes. The Rochford section was in West Street, opposite 'The Hollies', i.e., a house now called 'Danehurst'. Miss D. Blackwell and Miss C. Ingram were other teachers. The son of Dr. Emery, the daughter of

The Schools

S. C. Harris, retired clerk of the council, were pupils, when it was fee-paying. I saw a date on the wall of a bedroom at this house when I called in 1970, which I made out to be 1681. A smaller school still, called Spotland House began in 1937, and ran for nearly nine years. It was established at 64 Ashingdon Road and run by Mrs. T. G. Howard.

In the 20th century the very rapid increase in the population made the building of more schools necessary, so a secondary modern school was built in Rocheway in 1937. This moved to Boswell Avenue in 1961/2, mainly because of the noise problem from the nearby airport. This school became comprehensive in 1967 and is now called King Edmund school. Hawkwell Holt junior and infant school opened in 1957 for the children of the estate behind it when I was appointed headmaster. It split in 1962 after a new school had been built on the same field. The infants remained in their first abode, the juniors moved over to the new location. In 1965 the name was changed to the Holt Farm schools. Three years later a new junior school was built just off The Drive, called Doggetts, it being quite close to that farm.

Chapter Eleven

INDUSTRIES OF ROCHFORD

THERE WERE ONLY TWO potash industries recorded in the whole of Essex, and Rochford was one. This was run by Henry Townsend. It was recorded as on the east side of the road from Fambridge Ferry to Rochford. Whether this meant there was a road joining North Street running up The Drive, which has only been made recently, and so on across the fields to Ashingdon, or whether it meant the use of Ashingdon Road and Dalys Road to join up to North Street as now is not clear. I think the latter since Dalys Road is marked in some maps as Potash Lane, the one of 1895 so gives it. This could have placed the potash as somewhere on the spot now known as Reeve's Timber Yard, at the far end of North Street. Some of the wood used in its manufacture came from a copse almost opposite, now part of the hospital grounds, but most came from the woods facing the end of Rectory Road, where it joins the Hockley Road at Nursery Corner. These woods began behind The Lawn and carried on to Hockley Woods and beyond. They were called Potash Wood hereabouts. There was an old woodcutter who stayed in a small wooden hut, just behind 'Potash Cottages', where he lived for most of the year, cutting the wood up ready for the firing.

Mr. Townsend paid 5d. a bushel for good dry wood ash, although housewives kept their own very often to soften the hard water for washing, as they could ill afford soap.

Benton says that after the ashes were exhausted by drawing their lye, they were further used for manuring. Townsend and his son, Barnabas, ceased their business about 1850. The decline was caused by three factors, first the coming of the railway, which brought coal in quickly, so less wood was used anyway; cheap potash was also coming from abroad, especially South America; and, thirdly, an economical method of making soda from common salt was found.

In 1868 Meeson built three pairs of cottages for his workmen at the end of North Street on the east side. The first pair, near the bend into Malting Villas were pulled down about 1900. Mr. Reeve pulled down the middle pair to build his own bungalow there in 1959, whilst the front wall of his wood yard was part of the last pair. This was replaced in 1972 by a new wall further back.

The Gas Works

There is an estate office in East Street today (1973) close to where the gas works stood. They were constructed in 1845 by a limited company when W. T. Meeson was made chairman, and George Wood the solicitor, for the business. The Rochford Council had consented to the sale of the property for £250. Mr. Broadberry was its first manager when the price of the gas was 7s. 6d. per 1,000 cubic feet. John Church was in charge three years later, followed by Jabez Shelley in 1855. Richard Broadberry, son of the first-named was here in 1870, but John Cowling was given in 1874-86; then in 1890 John Hoult took over. W. Cowling, son of John, returned from Sussex to take the position before 1903,[1] when he was named and his spell continued for a long period until 1930. The last manager to hold the employment was Alfred Edward Jennings, who took over until it was dismantled. The works had four retorts and two other containers, one for tar and another for stores. In 1909,[2] Messrs. Samuel White and Son, Queen Victoria Street, London, held it.

The Brick and Tile Fields

On Friday, 2 August 1867, in a sale[3] at Tokenhouse Yard, near the Bank of England, a field was bought by William Daniels, who had rented it. This was a brickfield, partly in Rochford and partly in Stambridge. It was a field a short distance from where there is now a row of eight cottages, all under one roof, Nos. 103-117 Stambridge Road, which were made with bricks from this field. They were called 'Carey's Cottages', and were built for the workmen of the firm of Carey and Birch, steam plough works in Lingfield Drive. Arthur Carey's name was first shown in 1870, but Kelly in 1882 records the firm with the three partners, Carey, Stilwell, and Birch. It was Arthur Finnis Stilwell who joined the firm last, but he remained to carry on the business, which never really prospered and disappeared about 1892. Today the cottages have been re-named and are now called Russell Terrace.

The Cherry Orchard brickworks, off Hall Road, now a subsidiary of the larger Star Brick Company of Great Wakering, is a very old firm. Once it was a very prosperous yard, employing over 100 men, but today only about 30 are left. It was here that the traditional 'red' bricks were made which were used for many Rochford houses. These were hand-made, but most are machine done today, save for a few specials with shapes for walls, churches, or decorative styling. These have such fancy names as single and double bullnose, squints, saddles, dog leg, camt, splay, plinth header, etc. The clay is obtained from a field across the road from the works. The seam varies from a mere two inches to over seven feet. Although it has been worked for hundreds of years an estimate recently made reckoned there was enough material for another 150 years or more.

Fetherbys and Wests were two other brickfields in Rochford with some 40-odd men working in each. Mr. Pritchard was the manager of Fetherbys when the wages were only up to £3 per week for men working five and a half days with 10-12 hours daily. Wests made sandstone bricks, and much of Sutton Road and Sutton Court Drive was made with these. Wests, which closed about 1914, was further down Watts Lane than Fetherby's pit, although they both began around 1894. Both men came from Kent.

Two tile fields existed in the town. The first was on the left-hand side of Ark Lane, going in from Hall Road. About 25 yards down, taking the left-hand fork, there was a gate which led to the field. Just beyond and to the left again there are the remains of an old barn. I had this photographed in 1969, and although open in many places to the weather, it was still remarkably sound, with some solid wood, particularly the cross timbers, in one end. It was built in the early years of 1800 to dry roofing tiles so its sides were open to allow air to circulate. There were at least two brick cottages situated a few yards up the right-hand fork which were occupied by workmen from the manor estate of Rochford Hall. The barn was much used by down-and-outs in winter. It was usually called the Kiln Barn, but the name Tile Barn was also used. There is a peg-tile in Prittlewell Priory museum found during repairs to 19 South Street, with this inscription in old English: 'May the 22, 1777, Samuel Wellham at Studgreen near Rochford, made this tile'.

The other tile field was nearer to Rochford Hall. The two were called the Great and Little Kiln fields. The tiles from both fields found their way to many of the roofs of the better-class houses in and around Rochford. A glazed tile of the 13th-15th centuries found in a brickfield and now in the Prittlewell Priory museum like the above, probably came from one of these two tile fields.

The last brickfield in Rochford belonged to Thomas Sloman, a Westcliff builder, who purchased a field on Ashingdon Road in 1898[4] from the trustees of the late Dr. T. P. King. He bought an arable field of 11 acres for £700, and another piece of 6 acres 3 roods 18 perches for £190.[5] The first field was behind the row of houses named after him, six of which were built in 1900 when his own soft red bricks were used. The the second row of houses was built a little later, and the two were separated by a road leading to the brickworks. Today this is called Meeson's Mead, and has a small housing estate on it. It was on 11 September 1902[6] that Sloman requested permission to erect these further 20 houses, for his workers.

The Mills

The oldest type of windmill known was the post mill with the movable part fixed on a stout post, often a tree stump, cut off some four or five feet from the ground. Access to the mill was obtained by a long sloping ladder at the back, but this could also be used as an arm to turn the whole mill round to face the wind. A circular-roofed shed was later added round the post for storage. It was thus called the round house. Then mills were made with sails covered with canvas or linen fabric, but later thin wooden slats were used. In the 14th century tower mills were invented which had four sails, but some have been recorded with up to sixteen. The sails again varied in size from a length of 20 feet

Industries of Rochford

up to 50 feet. Such mills could turn a wind-wheel of several hundredweight.

There was a windmill mentioned in the charter given to Sir Guy de Rochford in 1247. In 1518 Sir Thomas Bullen had licence to carry 'wode billets from his mylle at Rochford'. There is no evidence as to its whereabouts, but the only hilly ground is Potash Hill where Rectory Road enters the present Hockley Road. In 1810 a post windmill was built by Thomas Scott in the garden of a house in South Street, formerly the residence of Mr. George Wood, but its duration was a bare four years, for in 1814 it was sold. Thomas Kemp, a miller at the tidal mill at Broomhills, about a mile away, bought it. He had it taken down and set up again in Little Stambridge, near his other mill, where it stood until around 1900. D. Smith[7] records an auction sale at the *King's Head* in 1814 by order of the trustees of Thomas Scott. The bill's particulars quoted several items, including lot 1: 'a piece of copy-hold ground containing approximately half rood of land with a most substantial, well-built and newly erected Post Windmill thereon, carrying two pairs of French stones and capable of grinding 50-60 quarters per week, eligibly situated in the market town of Rochford, in a fine corn country, and within a mile of a wharf from whence vessels sail weekly to London market'. This latter reference was to Broomhills and the Saturday barge which sailed to and from London dockyard. Harry Chapman gave me the location of this mill as the garden of what was the old council offices, used before by the Allens, father and son, builders and carpenters. The son married the daughter of T. L. Stagg, the baker. Harry used to work for Stagg and lived in his (Stagg's) back bedroom. He told me the baker often spoke of the mill and surely he would know. The shop in West Street, now owned by

Cramphorn, the seed merchants, used to be called Mill House. Its rear is on Back Lane, just a few yards away from a side entrance to the council yard.

There was another mill here in West Street, where the back of Warren's showroom is today. The garage was the workshop of Arthur Topsfield, the blacksmith, who had a cottage on the end. When his family grew, he purchased the adjoining cottage, which was called 'The Old Water Mill', as a stream that ran across the grounds of the old Union (workhouse) went under the end of the premises and across the street into the brook. Jack Topsfield, son of the above, told me that part of a wheel was found in 1902 and added, when talking to me in 1969, that one end of the house was very much lower than the remainder. He judged that this was where the mill wheel had worked.

Chapter Twelve

THE TRADERS OF ROCHFORD

BROWN DECLARED that between 1770 and 1775[1] there were seven general shops, three butchers and two bakers here, whilst between 1785 and 1788[2] the total had increased by six. The first directory of 1793[3] was also surprising in the number of trades and traders given, and it was here that I began my inventory.

Tailors

Thomas Kelly and Samuel Paprill were recorded on the Invasion returns of 1803[4] and they were joined in the first of Pigot's Directories for 1823/4 by John Aylett, who was here until 1855. In 1828[5] James Whittaker's name was mentioned, but he was here before that since on 7 June 1827[6] his shop was up for sale as lot 4, described as near the market place. Since he continued to 1835[7] it was assumed he purchased the business himself. John Raymond (1832-55) was one of the few whose place of work I could find, for he had the shop next to Giles, the banker, in the lower end of West Street, now numbered thirty-three. William Liddell was another from 1855 to 1878.

The name R. T. Hunt occurred in my story of the two murders. He had the shop in the market corner nearest to Connaught House, now numbered thirty. His dates were given as 1866-1900. A. S. Arnold started in the same year at his house on the east side of Ashingdon Road, just inside the hospital wall, quite close to where Dalys Road began. In 1890 W. W. Hockley came and took up tailoring in a big way, for at one time he employed four men and a boy in the upstairs rooms of the shop which Raymond had previously occupied. He also took over part of 'The Hollies', nearly opposite, as a kind of storeroom for cloth and finished articles, but later he removed to No. 12 in the Square, where he remained until 1910. Then these premises were taken over by Percy W. Smith, who was here until 1914, when S. Brown opened up, followed in turn by A. E. Watts and F. Young. Meanwhile, Arthur Roger, who had been an apprentice with Hockley, set up in business for himself, from 1914 to 1924, in the upstairs rooms of a confectioner's shop in North Street, opposite the Congregational church. There was only one tailor left in Rochford, F. Benson, who began in 1936 on Stambridge Road. The business closed in 1972 after his death.

Drapers

Noble recorded the sale on Thursday, 10 December 1869, by Alfred Rodd, auctioneer, of several properties. Lot 1 was the drapery of William Payne, who bought it in for £700, and which stood on the corner of South Street and West Street. However, it was in this trade that Rochford had some famous men. A long-established firm was that of Bentall and Marsh, who had premises in South Street called Cromwell House, which was divided into two. In one they lived, in the other had their business. Begun in 1832, they continued to 1845, when the name G. Marsh appears alone and remained so to 1862. It then became Mills and Marsh until 1870, then Mrs. Marsh's name remained to 1878. Francis, the printer, said, 'I have seen four or five carriages at a time outside the drapery of Mr. Marsh in South street'.

The Traders of Rochford

An even more famous owner was George Winterbon, whose shop was on the north side of West Street, where Stanwood's wireless shop is today, he being first listed in 1828. So good were his clothes that people came from miles around, driving to the Square in pony and trap, horse and cart, or coming on foot. Even Brightwell of Southend sent his best customers to the store for bonnets, and such items of haberdashery. When he died in 1893 his wife carried on the business for a few years, then Fairhead, the assistant, took over until 1910.

On the opposite side to Marsh, W. Barnes had set up his shop much later, for his spell was from 1890 to 1937 in the place that had been G. Popplewell's building. There was one more long-established firm to record, for in 1859 W. Bishop came, taking over Payne's shop. He carried on with his sons and daughters and their children too, until 1955, by which time the family held five shops.

Ironmongers

One of the most interesting facts I found about the people of the town was their willingness, readiness or ability, call it what you will, to run not just one trade, but two or more. Take the case of Thomas Quy, whom Pigot recorded first in 1823/4, whose shop was at the top of South Street. He doubled in the trade of auctioneer, but his trade bills declared he sold many things. William's name appeared in 1932, and with his two sons, the hardware trade was carried on to 1908. The Cowling brothers followed them up to 1946, when the present owner, W. C. E. Ling, took over.

J. D. Garrood's name has been mentioned before as postmaster and water carrier, but he also dealt in cane-work and basketry. His was named as ironmonger in 1862, and was in the 1890 directory, but his wife carried on, as many others did, when their husbands passed away. Of later years was the firm of Rome and Bishop, for when Asbey, the plumber, died in 1892, his wife carried on for nearly 10 years before finally selling to Arthur Bishop. Rome, who had come from Burnham as apprentice to Asbey, stayed on as Bishop's partner. The firm's name still survived in the Square until 1972, when they gave up.

Saddlers

The directory of 1793 listed George Burrows as an early saddler, but it was thought possible that the shop in the Square with the date 1777, was opened by him. However, since his name remained until 1862,[8] it was possible that his son followed him, having the same initials. Then came Robert Goodman and his son, who continued until 1919. In the next year Arthur Gridley came, but his stay was shorter, for he retired in 1943 after he had opened a branch shop to sell leather goods in West Street, where the wireless and electrics shop is today.

T. McBryer came in 1882 to the last shop in West Street on the north side. Later his son, Duncan, joined him, and he carried on alone when his father died. He finished in 1951.[9]

Blacksmiths

Two very early names in this field were those of Isaac Clark and John Burgess, both given in 1793. The former continued until 1848, when George's name appeared. This was his son, who remained until 1874 in their premises off Union Lane. The 1803 returns furnished the names of the Codling brothers, Thomas, Francis, and Edmond, in the trade, plus that of William Cottee, though I found him listed later as a farrier. At least one of the Codlings, George, lasted up to 1839 in their workshop in East Street, opposite to Weir Pond Road.

Another long-established firm was that of Whittingham, begun in a small shop in front of Clarks by 1830. Joseph was born in 1806 and after he opened the premises, he soon added to them with a foundry and then a carpenter's business, which he bought in, for he branched out to make not only the paraphernalia of a blacksmith, but also carts, gigs, and traps. All of these were made at the works where he employed four men in the ironwork, two men as carpenters, and several boys at odd times of the day. Barker, Whitby and Topsfield were three of the early smiths, and William Goodwin on the woodwork side.

Later still coaches, charabancs and bodies for cars were made with the firm doing all the work themselves. They had used iron-banded wheels and carts having iron supports for the sides in the beginning, but later used only wood. Whittingham was said to have been the first to introduce cross-benching on coaches and charabancs, at least in these parts, by means of which more passengers were carried. In 1968, Peter Whittingham[10] showed me a bill of sale dated 1890 which gave the price for a horse-drawn coach as £125 for a 20-seater, £130 for 25 people, and £140 for one to hold 30 persons. It was at these works that the first motor car to have a wooden body was made on 10 January 1903[11] for Dr. Silver Jones of 37 High Street, Southend.

Work began very early in the morning, for boys came at four o'clock to light the fires for the blacksmiths, who arrived half an hour later. Often as many as 150 shoes were put on to horses (left after the Thursday market) between five o'clock on Friday morning and midday on Thursday. A pin of beer (four and a half gallons) was placed in a small side room with a bite of bread and cheese for customers waiting their turn. Thursday was always a busy day, for apart from market buyers, it was melting-down day for the iron kept and scrap brought in.

In 1832 George Beard also began as a smith with his foundry on the other side of Union Lane, and he carried on to around 1870 when his wife had charge of the work, but with her son in the forge. Then Arthur Topsfield, who had bought the business for £5 down with the rest to pay, walked to Chelmsford to board a train to Colchester. There he borrowed £50 from his brother before he returned by the same method. To this he added his own savings to make up the required amount. Arthur was born on 30 January 1869 and died in 1934. He was highly regarded as an apprentice, being very careful at his work, and became a craftsman. He, in turn, trained several men who did well for themselves later on: there was William Flatman, George Downes, who set up later at Ingatestone, George and William Harris, and Harry Kemp. The latter joined the London police, whilst another, Tom Cunningham, went into the Hussars as a farrier. Jack Topsfield[12] joined his father in 1914 and retired in 1945. Topsfield senior had bought two cottages on the end of his workshop, and in 1888 pulled the wall down between them to make one large house. As they were largely built of ships' timbers this was an easy task, but it also proved a fire hazard and a few years afterwards such a catastrophe occurred. Fortunately, both men were alerted early and contained the blaze, but one huge beam over the fireplace had to be pulled clear. This proved no easy task as it was 15 feet long and almost a foot square. A cabinet-maker took it for use, but returned it as it proved too hard to work, so it was left in the yard to weather, and finally broken up with wedges and a sledge-hammer. Jack Topsfield, who was still alive in 1972, gave me most of these details.

Wheelwrights

Where there were blacksmiths so were there wheelwrights, the first of whom was John Freeman in 1793,[13] with William's name from 1832, and a Thomas of that family from 1855. They had a business in Wakering also. It seems that the two blacksmiths named did most of this work the next 30-40 years, since no wheelwrights are named until 1890, when George Tasker's name appeared. He had his works in South Street, opposite the old County Court, later the council offices. When I inspected the back premises in 1968 there was a large shed with a few old tools and a couple of completed wheels left hanging from rafters. Tasker used the front room of his house as an ironmonger's shop and remained up to 1948. He had originally come from Kent to work in the plough factory of Carey, Stilwell and Birch, but then began on his own. A. Hurrell senior, who was born in 1880, went to work for him on his 17th birthday and later carried on the business.[14]

Candlemakers

This, too, was a long-established trade with a small workshop behind the Square. Access to it was from the lane off North Street by the side of today's post office. Pritchard was the first maker, and Francis, the printer, wrote,[15] 'I suppose all the tallow candles in Rochford were made for Gillingham, the grocer'. However, when F. Scott took over the shop in 1862 he employed Martin Diss, whose home was in Asplin Terrace. The fat was melted down in a large iron pan after it had been collected from slaughter houses in and around the town. Monday was his melting day, and many were the complaints of the bad smell, but little was done about it. Mann was singled out as the culprit on 15 May 1888, but there were other times when he was cautioned. The hot fat was run off into other tubs for storage when too much was obtained. Cotton wicks were dipped into the wax up to 30 times, then cooled, to obtain the correct thickness. Smaller ones were sold cheaply as farthing dips. Chalk was thrown on the floor to prevent slipping, and customers were supposed to coat their shoes in a tray kept near the door. The remainder of the fat went to Messrs. Vanderberg's barges at Southend, and so to London by sea. The tubs were easily placed on the special cart made for the purpose: this was one of those burnt at the Mafeking celebrations. Martin Diss was a character,[16] noted for his very long finger nails, the laconic way he spoke, and for his accuracy with a gun, for he got frequent practice by shooting the rats which infested the works.

Chapter Thirteen

MORE ROCHFORD TRADERS

Butchers

CERTAIN SHOPS CARRIED on in the same trade for many years, often as a family concern. Such was the butchery of Stock, for Joseph was here in the Square in 1832,[1] whilst his son followed on from 1859 to 1890.[2] James Rutterford continued in the same shop to 1914 when A. Fance took over up to 1970. Another Stock, William, was a brother of Joseph and had a butcher's store in West Street, although he did not begin until 1859, and he was followed by his son, Walter, from 1870: Jabez Francis recalled him in his book.[3] These Stocks carried on until Charles Fordham took over in 1890, followed in turn by William Bradford in 1908, who had only a short stay, for William Henry Turner arrived in 1914 and remained until 1937.[4] He was the one who had stables and a small field behind 'Sloman's Cottages' on Ashingdon Road.

The retailers at the junction of East and North Streets had been in the trade for many years, for Geoffrey Webster sold meat to the Union as early as 21 December 1869,[5] and carried on until 1888 when William Palmer, who already had a shop some distance away in North Street, bought the business. He, too, had a son, Walter, who followed in his father's footsteps up to 1938, when A. Horner acceded, and he remained there until 1972 when he removed the whole business to the Square in Fance's old shop. Horner's old shop had been boarded up, but the intention is to make this into a new public library. In North Street was the establishment of W. Warren, recorded by Kelly in 1851,[6] but the name was changed to J. Warren thereafter up to 1886, when C. Warren appeared briefly on the scene. Their shop was on the left-hand corner of Market Alley. Lower down, on the same side, was the firm of J. and C. Searles, begun in 1908 with C. F. Searles in charge from 1916 to 1946, when A. Ferguson took over.

There were earlier butchers than all these, but it has proved difficult to find their whereabouts. James Thorne (1793-1832), John Thorne (1832-51), Thomas Cause (1845-1867), and William Hart (1859-1974) were such. Robert Turner,[7] I found, had a shop at the end of Barrack Lane, next to the *Marlborough Head* from 1832 to 1840, and Charles Horsnell's place,[8] with similar dates, was in South Street at the entrance to the wheelwright's yard.

Bakers

All of the four main streets of the town had long-established bakeries, an example of which was East Street, where Anne Dissmore was making bread from 1793.[9] The shop was by the side of the *New Ship* and continued later right across to North Street, and she was followed by the brothers J. and W. Harvey to 1845, when Mrs. Harvey's name was found, until she was relieved by her son from 1851 to 1855. In North Street, next to the present post office, William Clark started from 1803[10] to 1848. Next Thomas Popplewell took over the shop for a lengthy spell from 1860 to 1886. Samuel Fuller was its next occupant from 1900 to 1916, with E. Minett there for the next 10 years, followed by Hedley Coates for 12 years, with its last occupier, A. J. Arthy, who finally gave up in 1959.

More Rochford Traders

At the corner of Back Lane and South Street is A. J. Arthy's second shop. John Coe began here in 1823, and he had a stay of nearly 40 years, and was then succeeded by George Playle. This name continued for a very long spell, but it was run by A. G. Playle from 1895 to 1910, when Mrs. Playle took over for the war years, 1914-1918. Finally Arthy came just before 1922. A few yards down the street is a newsagent's shop which was formerly the bakery of W. Lancaster from 1851 to 1878, with T. F. Howard, who followed from 1890 to 1896.

Many postcards are still in the hands of the older generation of Rochford folk with the Square being shown with the old pump and a baker's shop on the east side, just before turning into the alley. This clearly advertised that it was established in 1825. Abraham Ling's name was given as the baker, although directories only recorded him from 1832. Again, his stay was a long one, until Mrs. Ling's name came from 1874 up to 1895. She was renowned for her brandy snaps and a confection that rejoiced in the name parliament cake. George Davies followed her in the trade to approximately 1917, after which it became known as West's Tearooms, and so remained until that side of the Square was remodelled.

North Street had another baker of some renown named Thomas Lewin Stagg, an eccentric if ever there was one, or perhaps he was a self-contained advertising agent. He would ask several millers to deliver flour on the same day, and he always wore a white top hat. When, on one occasion, J. Cowling, the gas manager, came to read the meter, he looked under the counter for the installation. Stagg asked what he was doing, whereupon Cowling answered, 'I am looking for the coppers you throw there'. Quick as a flash, Stagg, who was reputed to do this, replied, 'I've just sacked them up for the bank'. I am indebted to Harry Chapman for this story, true, I am sure, since he worked as a boy for the baker and lived over the shop for a while.

Grocers

Here again, I found evidence of a man who engaged in several trades, for William White Gillingham's bills advertised him in this trade together with those of tea-dealer, cheese-monger, tallow-chandler, also glass and china. He was born in 1800 and died in 1875, having his house on the north side of the Square at the west corner, and his shop on the other end, next to the alley. The business was carried on by H. Scott until the fire of 1884, when he removed to West Street. In South Street were the premises of William Gower, in a building called Cromwell House, which was later divided into two and numbered nine and 11 respectively. Benton said that he was noted for the quality of his provisions and was respected as an upright trader.[11] W. Francis said he kept two or three vans going to supply people in Southend.[12] His wife continued to serve the people and delivered to the Union in 1873. H. Simms took over the shop until 1889 when he transferred to 51 West Street. Cromwell House was unexpectedly pulled down in December 1970, after it had been empty some years.

I have written about Shelley in the Square, again a grocer of long standing, who started before 1875. Its name continued until the alterations in November 1961, but it was run by its former manager, Starkins, for its last years. Thomas McDurmid, who died 20 February 1869, was here in the same trade before Shelley. However, an earlier grocer still was William LeGrys, who had the shop[13] at the corner of Old Ship Lane opposite that public house before 1823. In 1870 John Potter came, followed by his son, John Starnes

Potter until 1932. Another son, Innifer, has an ironmongery in Hockley today.

Watchmakers

Rochford can proudly boast of some famous men in this trade, one of the best being Francis Furner, who was here before 1794.[14] Samples of his craft fetch high prices today; some specimens were kept in the Chelmsford Museum but were stolen recently. His son, who was apprenticed on 7 April 1794 to Richard Simner of Old Street, London, for the sum of £30, was recorded up to 1859. On his return to Rochford, he set up in the second house in the Market Alley, on the right-hand side entering from North Street. This was said to be the darkest house in the town, for it had but a small window and looked out across the lane to a very large high chimney. The ceiling was only six feet high, and the room dropped some nine inches to the floor on entry. Further light was provided by candles, and later by an oil lamp. His father had part of 'The Hollies', now numbered 48, but it is not known if this was a shop or residence.

John Gullock, shown in the 1793 directory[15] had a son, Philip Hoare Gullock, listed in the 1803 returns, by which it must be clear the father was in the trade well before the earliest date given, whilst the son carried on to 1848. Another was Charles 'Manny' Carter listed by Pigot in 1832-51, who also had a relative, Nathaniel, who continued in the trade from 1900 to 1955, whose fame could very well rest upon the fact that he was the last known man in Essex to make watches. His first shop was the one on the corner of West and North Streets, where a window jutted out on to the path. When T. Offin left from the shop on the opposite corner he moved across. George Naunton was another who excelled in the occupation. The Post Office

Directory for 1859 first documents him, but he was here earlier as he presented a bill for re-winding the town clock, dated 10 April 1854.[16] His shop was the one Carter later occupied.

There were others in the same field, perhaps not so well known, as for example, James Underwood, whose office was next to the Women's Institute in West Street. He was more of a clockmaker, so made a good job of the town's clocks and those of the Union as on 7 October 1889.[17] Also J. Spurge (1855-59) and Peter Davey (1763-65),[18] of whom little was found, but one with something to sing about was surely J. Day, given as here from 1902. In 1910[19] he composed a new national anthem, which he sent to King George, who graciously acknowledged it. His shop was next to that of McBryer, the saddler, at the end of West Street, north side.

Bootmakers

I mean no shame in putting this trade near the end, for there were men here who should be called craftsmen. I name three whose skill was vouched for by Harry Chapman; the first being John White, whose name was taken from the 1823/4 Directory, and which persisted to the 1886 guide book. He lived and worked in a small house in South Street on one side of the Manse, where he employed four men. Later the shop became a ladies' hairdressers, but has been empty for many years. William Bowell is the second skilled workman, and his, too, was a small house at the end of Asplin Terrace, nearest to the *Rose and Crown*. He appeared in Kelly's *Directory* for 1878, and continued up to 1914. Besides his primary skill, he was also a good musician, able to play most stringed and wind instruments. He taught the violin to several people, including Harry Chapman. The

CHRISTMAS NOVELTIES!!!

✳ ✳ ✳ ✳ ✳ ✳ ✳ ✳ ✳

IF YOU WANT

A LARGE ASSORTMENT OF **XMAS PRESENTS** TO SELECT FROM
GO TO

HEDGECOCK'S

OPPOSITE THE COUNTY COURT,
HIGH STREET, ROCHFORD,
where you may see an immense quantity of

DRESSED DOLLS from 1d. each,
XMAS CARDS FROM 2D. PER DOZEN,
BIRTHDAY CARDS, 10 IN A PACKET, FOR ONE PENNY,
XMAS CARDS WITH SILK FRINGE 2D. EACH,
(These are Marvellously Cheap.)

Christmas Tree Ornaments almost innumerable!!
FANCY NEEDLEWORK OF ALL KINDS,
BERLIN WOOLS IN ALL SHADES 4/6 PER POUND,
SCOTCH YARNS FROM 1D. PER OZ.
The New China Vases in a variety of shapes, from 4½d. each.
FOOT-OTTOMANS FOR NEEDLEWORK TOPS,
Work Boxes, Writing Desks, Ink Stands, Mirrors, Glove and Handkerchief Boxes,
AND

TOYS IN ENDLESS VARIETY.

J. FRANCIS AND SONS, STEAM PRINTERS, ROCHFORD.

Fig. 5 Handbill of the Haberdashery, *c.* 1885

third person was James Hedgecock, who lived at 17 South Street. It had two bow windows projecting on to the path. In one sat James at his work; in the other, his wife, who was an accomplished needlewoman. The years 1855-95 were his given dates. The handbill (Fig. 5) gives a clear idea of their handiwork as well as a sidelight on the life of the times, c. 1885. The Invasion returns of 1803 included the name of John Newman, who held on to his trade to 1867, who was concerned with the sale of his shop on West Street's south side on 7 June 1827.[20]

Plumbers

In the chapter on Water, and the one on the Great Fire, I have written of Robert Asbey of the Square. He kept a shop in the centre of the north side, where he sold paint and paraffin as well as articles of his trade. His stay in Rochford was a long one, 1823-1886, whilst his wife carried on from that date to 1900. Fred Crowe, who had been his assistant, took over the *Golden Lion* in 1887, but did odd-jobbing as well. His son, also named Fred, carried on for a while, but then continued more as a glazier up to 1914.

I have chosen the following tale to end my story of the traders of the town, told to me by 'Chick' Robinson, the signwriter and grainer of East Street. He said, 'I had to go on the roof of Shelley's in 1953 to renew some old lead flashing. On one of the sheets near the chimney I found the footprints of Fred Crowe's son, marked on the lead by a series of dots made with a bradawl. In one of the impressions the date 1853 had been chased, in the other were a couple of lines of poetry. These were from Omar Khayyam, 'The moving finger writes; And having writ, moves on'. What a coincidence with exactly 100 years between the happening.

Chapter Fourteen

THE TWO MURDERS

IF THE CASE-BOOKS were searched it would prove difficult to find a pair of murders with such different stories, for one was a mystery that is still unsolved, and yet the file can certainly be considered closed: the other unrivalled for the callousness displayed.

The first evolved in the quiet of a sunny summer afternoon where a lonely thicket was the scene of the crime. This was the spot, halfway across what is now the Rochford Hundred golf club, but in the great days of the Hall, was a bigger copse kept for game, where the body was found. It was described by a youth named Alfred Hazel who discovered the body: 'As I approached the Wilderness, all was quiet and peaceful. When I got to the middle of the waste, I saw a woman lying on the ground. At first I thought she was resting or was asleep, but something about her position made me go closer. I then saw she had cuts on her throat and her head was lying almost in the stream. Bending down to look more closely I touched her and got blood on my hands. I became afraid and wiped them on my jacket and turning round, fled, back the way I had come and ran all the way up to West street until I was breathless'.

He was seen in the street by shopkeepers and passersby, who informed the police when information was sought. Few signs of a struggle were found; only a broken umbrella bore witness to a fight. Alfred was apprehended by Superintendent Samuel Hawtree on 10 June 1893[1] and accused of murder. He was allowed to go free, and later that evening talked with Harry Chapman, who knew him well, as they were schoolmates. Harry told me that all his statements were checked and found to agree with his story. Harry declared, 'I am quite sure he did not commit the crime, he was so matter of fact, about the whole thing'. Indeed, only four days later Alfred was discharged.

The woman turned out to be Mrs. Emma Hunt, whose husband was a tailor and lived in the second house of three which stood next to the *Old Ship*, now its car park. The murder, as I said, was not solved, but comment after the deed disclosed a curious fact. Mrs. Hunt had made a habit of walking down the Hall Road for some time, a fact noticed by various people. It was said she had done so twice on the previous day; it was likewise stated that she was on more than friendly terms with another man. Was this true? Did the fact that she went twice have a significance? Was a meeting arranged at which he failed to appear so that she returned the following day? Could this have led to words, then blows? One could go on — guessing perhaps on these scanty trifles that were probably exaggerated and were most certainly investigated.

My second story is crystal clear, for the murderer was known from the instant the deed was committed. The cause was equally plain and so very trivial. A man named Wilkes, who lived near Pudsey Hall, a mile from Canewdon, was in the habit of sending his wife every Thursday morning to Rochford market for some tobacco. This task she had performed faithfully for many a month without mishap, but on this occasion she had been prevented from reaching the shop in time so that her usual purchase of half a pound of loose tobacco had not been made.

She was a woman of medium build, quiet and well spoken, but long in fear of her dominant husband, for he was both tall and powerfully built, with a large black beard, and a temper to match. Picture the scene: the woman, trembling and nervous all the way home, who approached her gate with trepidation, perhaps even with premonition. There she paused, hand on the latch, whereat her husband, already angry at her delay, shouted to her to hurry. Then he recognised from her expression that something was amiss, and met her halfway down the path, swearing and cursing already. She began to stammer her story, but he, in fury, would hear none of it, but rained blows on her, until finally she fell to the ground, where he vented his rage still further by kicking her until finally death ensued. Wilkes awaited the law calmly and walked unhesitatingly to the police station where the enormity of his offence then became apparent to him. He motioned Inspector Chase to open the door for him and as the officer did so, he wheeled around and fled down the street before he turned into Weir Pond Road. He was caught by the legs when he attempted to slither under a gate at the far end, a way that led to open fields across to the river Crouch and possible freedom. The man who caught him, by a strange quirk of fate, was named Hazell.

Chapter Fifteen

THE POLICE

MOST OF THE ACCOUNTS we have of disorder in the county of Essex and Rochford in particular were obtained from petty sessions and quarter sessions records and other files at the Essex Record Office in Chelmsford. It is from these we know that law and order was being kept by a kind of paid system of constables and high constables. Such was Jonah or Jonas Monk, recorded in 1653 as one of those paying homage at the Whispering Court for a farm called the Moat and Springs, near to Rochford. He was also named in the court rolls of the Manor of Rochford Hall. He died in 1677 and he was counted in the Hearth Tax list of 1671[1] where he was quoted as having four hearths. His will[2] at the office was a lengthy document wherein several Rochford people were mentioned, and they included, 'his loving friend Otto Proctor', who was a magistrate of the town. An early reference to him as a constable was in 1653,[3] but two years later, on 11 August 1655[4] Henry Berryman and Henry Dates were given as high constables for the area. On 26 July 1671,[5] 15 July 1672,[6] and in 1673,[7] Monke was named with William Stevens as high constables for the Hundred. In that last year he was given as infirm. Later the Hundred was guarded and protected by other paid officials, in Rochford's case this was stated to be by 51 peace officers and two protection societies. There is a volume, dated 1879,[8] in care at Chelmsford, of the Rochford and Dengie Hundred Association for the prosecution of felons, and a further document of the original articles of the 16 members which were concluded at the *Old Ship* on 26 November of that year.[9]

However, I am indebted to F. G. Emmison[10] from his book on Elizabethan disorder for the following five accounts: that of an assault on John Cooke, gentleman of Rochford, his wife and ward in 1572[11] by John Pylborowe and three yeoman, all of Hatfield Peverel; that at the quarter sessions of 1587,[12] William Folkes, a Rochford Yeoman took out a chancery writ against Joseph Berrie of Eastwood, gentleman, fearing bodily harm and arson; that in 1590[13] Richard Peverel, another yeoman of the town was bound over to answer a charge of stealing conies [rabbits], 'if in the meantime my Lady Rich [of Rochford Hall] do not release him'; again in 1597[14] when four Rochford men passed off a 12d. coin as worth 12s., when one was found guilty of uttering and was whipped and pilloried, one was acquitted, and the others absconded; and lastly, a case of common assault took place in 1602[15] where Elizabeth, wife of Henry Cannoudon, the local blacksmith beat Margery, wife of Walter Samon there.

Stephen Jackson, born in 1654, and lessee of Great Doggett's farm was high constable for the Hundred until his death on 24 December 1706, and he was followed some time later by Thomas Salmon, a Rochford shopkeeper, who held the title for a span, which included the years 1825 to 1829.[16] In 1761 Rochford and Prittlewell were beset by a gang of seamen who had been prisoners of war in France, and came here begging relief.

The next year, on 10 April,[17] following other corn riots in Essex, eight persons of Rochford were arraigned against the King, when Backhouse Carr (of 'The Lawn'), a magistrate, was called as one of the witnesses for the prosecution.

In 1763 John Rivers, alias Aaron Springfield, of the town of Rochford, was executed for burglary: truly a sign of the hard times. On 13 January 1774[18] John Briggs, constable of the town sent in his bill for attendance at the Epiphany Sessions, held at Chelmsford, when legal proceedings were taken against William Matthew for uttering counterfeit coins.

A different case was the letter of 3 May 1737,[19] signed by Thomas Scratton and R. Salmon, churchwardens, Canon Barrington, and William Everett, overseers, Edmond Digby and Simon Craske, constables, to all owners of property in the town, warning of the grave dangers of taking in lodgers because of the risks of smallpox. Late in the 18th century and early in the next we find evidence that overseers had begun to assume the duties of constables in their areas. An example was the proclamation of George Winterbon, draper and overseer, who wrote to the constables of Essex that George Gray of this town had deserted his wife. John Barrington of Great Doggetts signed the letter, dated 8 August 1829.[20] In the compilation of the Invasion returns for 1803 the report for the town was signed by Edward Codlin and John Wade, constables, but we know from the 1793 Directory that Codlin was a tinsmith, while a Samuel Wade was listed as licensee of the *New Ship*, and a William Wade was registered as a carpenter. Another case with a difference was the declaration of Sarah Richmond, who married Henry Townsend in 1812,[21] she being his second wife. The dispute was over property, but there was an added twist in the statement, 'that not one of my husband's children lived to be more than a few weeks old, . . . my husband was buried in 1835 . . . my own daughter, named Sarah was baptised by her uncle, without my consent and is now a servant with Mr. Vanderzee of 3 Francis Terrace, Kentish Town'. Mrs. Townsend had property called

The Police

'Mountain House' in Rochford. It is believed Henry and Charles Townsend had connections with the *White Horse*. Further evidence of the severity of sentences was given for 13 March 1828, when Dr. Grabham's maid was deported for seven years for stealing from him.

When the Essex police force was properly constituted in 1840, Rochford was allowed two constables, and Southend one. Thomas Noakes was an early constable, for he joined on 21 May 1840, whilst Samuel Sealbrook, who signed on a few months later in November, was sent to keep him company, but by January 1846 he was serving here as inspector. Superintendent Algernon William Low, who began his career on 3 June 1841 at Rayleigh, came to Rochford in his rank when the police station was built in North Street, where he still had but two constables. He left on 31 August 1850, when Superintendent Flood, who joined the force on 6 December 1842, came to take over after being an inspector at Southend.

At the Lent Assizes in 1841, Joseph Griggs, aged 24, who had stolen an ewe from Thomas Sach, was arrested by Low; convicted by the court, he was sentenced to transportation for 14 years. In 1840, Uriah Kent, a small farmer here, had his house burgled when five sovereigns were taken. At the Chelmsford Assizes on 22 July, three prisoners were sentenced to death for the crime, but the judge, Lord Abinger, said they would probably be transported for life. A similar robbery occurred about 1890 when Tom Shepherd, who lived in a house fronting on Ashington Road, on the corner of Roche Avenue, had his savings stolen from him. He had been in the habit of storing them in a red handkerchief which he stuffed up the chimney in a special cavity. He changed his money to gold whenever he had accumulated enough, and at the time of the offence declared he had 80 gold coins. After several days an anonymous tip-off enabled the police to recover most of the sum from a hole in Tinker's Lane. It was thought at the time that the thief or thieves were scared at the large number of coins and their tell-tale amount.

Benton[23] records Sergeant Turner, who died in 1854, was a noted constable and thief-taker, whilst another well-known policeman was Sergeant James Watson, who left a case-book of notes[24] which gave instances of crime for the last decade of the 19th century. About 1900 quite a commotion broke the peace in the Square one afternoon. It happened when four of Cottis's men who had finished loading a barge at Stambridge mill earlier than expected, walked to Rochford to celebrate. They chose the *King's Head* to do this, but after consuming several drinks, became noisy, whereupon the barman asked them to be quiet or he would have to put them out. They in turn, proceeded to do just that, to him. P.c. Smith was near the market and heard the noise so came over and called for peace. By this time, fearing neither friend nor foe, the four men began to manhandle him also, and the fight continued across the Square. James Rutterford, the butcher, endeavoured to assist the constable, but was laid low by a blow in the stomach. The noise was heard by Inspector Chase in the station, who sallied out and managed to handcuff one of the miscreants. No sooner was this done than the man staggered to his feet and brought his fetters down hard on the town pump which snapped them. The fracas continued on and down into West Street, but with the assistance of some of the shopkeepers there, the men were eventually subdued. At the subsequent trial, two were sent to prison, and two others, believed to be 'Trout' Webb and a man named Livermore, were fined.

The Police

Inspector Chase, whose name occurs in several chapters, had a long stay here. The Essex constabulary, who kindly furnished me with the dates given for members of the force, told me he had almost 40 years of service from 11 September 1865 to 31 March 1902. In his later days he was promoted to Superintendent and despite several mishaps, he received many commendations for his work. Once[25] when checking the vagrants at the shed behind the *Rose and Crown,* he put his foot under a body to roll the supposed man over to see his face. The next moment he found himself in the grip of a brown bear, sleeping next to his master. The bear gave performances in the Square, where he was a well-known sight. It was said he would not pass the *Horse and Groom* until he was given a glass of beer. Chase became relieving officer for the town for nine years after his retirement.

The Police Station

On 16 December 1840[26] the Clerk of the Peace for Essex had communicated his wishes to Michael Comport, solicitor of Rochford regarding the purchase of a piece of land for a police station, but it was not until several years later that anything happened. Plans were finally drawn up on 1 February 1847[27] and agreed on 19 April of that year when the land was eventually bought from George Wood, another solicitor. Charles Carter, a builder from South Street, who had submitted the plan and an estimate of £803 13s. was chosen to build it. The date and his name were cut in the facia board under the guttering on the front of the building and remained there for many years, until in 1966, when it was modernised by Muggleton, a builder from Ashingdon Road. It had become the post office by this time and a new station for the police was built in South Street, near to Salt Bridge in 1916.

Chapter Sixteen

THE WORKHOUSE, THE ALMSHOUSES AND OTHER CHARITIES

POOR LAW RELIEF prior to 1597 was by almsgiving, the guilds, the parish and the church. Webb[1] said in that year a statute was made requiring overseers of the poor and churchwardens to provide for the destitute. In 1598 the Justices for Essex made orders for the poor with one principal house at Coggleshall and 24 sub-houses in other parts of the county. In 1638 a body called the Commissioners for the Poor was set up, but a standstill occurred after that[2] and only non-able bodied persons were helped, and that only if they were of the parish, others being whipped and sent packing.[3] Beggars were outlawed, many branded, but the problem remained. In the last quarter of the 17th century Richard Haines proposed the creation of unions like those of Holland. Instead, rising poor rates and a myriad of vagrants led to various reports such as the one in 1697 by John Locke[4] who proposed such persons be employed at lower rates. Recruitment was advocated as a remedy, but in general the old-fashioned methods of whipping and the stocks were used. The Poor Law Amendment Act of 1834 was a great spur to a more lasting improvement. However, many parishes and rural districts had already begun to move in the matter, and either separately or in combination, had superseded the old poor

The Workhouse, the Almshouses and Other Charities

houses or free shelters with an organised workhouse.[5] In fact Prittlewell had such a place in 1728, but Rochford's appeared later, for Thomas Gepps and his wife were appointed master and matron of a House of Industry on 18 April 1774.[6] The immates had to spin and card wool in the place which had five rooms, plus a buttery, brewhouse and spinning room. On 21 May 1775 Thomas Wakelin was given leave to farm the land round the house[7] helped by the inmates.

On 19 May 1800,[8] Thomas Allen drew up plans to build a pauper institution, but it was not dealt with immediately since he agreed to be paid the cost, some 200 guineas, in two instalments in 1808 and 1809.[9] This was the place on the Southend Road just outside the parish, and stood on the corner of Queen Elizabeth's Chase and consisted of a master's house with three small dwellings adjoining. These were bought by Daniel Scratton of the Priory of Prittlewell who used them for his workmen when the 'Union' was built in the town. The master signing the weekly slips, for payment by the overseers, was William Salmon for the period 27 June 1823 to March 1824, but William Claydon's name was given in April 1829.[10] Essex Record Office have a list of clothing of the inmates for that year[11] which showed the sparseness of their outfit. This listed boys of the ages of three, six and seven, girls of seven, and adults of 17, 60, 63, 67, 70, 72, and 77 as in the house.

In 1834 a number of Essex parishes were asked if they possessed a workhouse and who were its chief inmates.[12] Rochford replied in the affirmative and reported its inmates as chiefly old and infirm people, also the children of convicts, with six men between the ages of 60-82, six boys, 4-14 years old, and two women, aged 24 and 43 respectively. Their diet was given as bread, potatoes, tea and milk, with

THE WORKHOUSE

MENU 1843

	No. 1 Generous Diet	No. 2 Low Diet	No. 3
Breakfast	1 pt Tea, 4 oz B/B	Same	The
Dinner	6 oz Meat, 4 oz Bread, 1 lb Potato	8 oz Rice or Batter Pudding	Common
Supper	1 pt Tea, 4 oz B/B	Same	Diet

Cost of able-bodied paupers is 1s 5½d per week: Cost of Officer Establishment exceeds a double ration of a pauper by 8d per week, i.e. . . . is 3s 7d each.

15 August 1843

MENU 1893
Approved by Local Government Board 29 September 1893
Adopted by Rochford 31 December 1893

Menu A For able-bodied men and women

Day	Breakfast		Dinner					Supper			
	Bread	Gruel	Bread	Meat	Potato	Broth	Suet Pudding	Bread	Cheese	Gruel	Tea or Broth
S Men	6 oz	1½ pt	3 oz	4 oz	12 oz	—	—	6 oz	1 oz	1 pt	—
Wmn	5 oz	1½ pt	3 oz	4 oz	12 oz	—	—	5 oz	1 oz	1 pt	—
M	6 oz	1½ pt	4 oz	—	—	1½ pt	—	6 oz	1 oz	—	1 pt
	5 oz	1½ pt	4 oz	—	—	1½ pt	—	5 oz	1 oz	—	1 pt
T	6 oz	1½ pt	3 oz	4 oz	12 oz	—	—	6 oz	1 oz	1 pt	—
	5 oz	1½ pt	3 oz	4 oz	12 oz	—	—	5 oz	1 oz	1 pt	—
W	6 oz	1½ pt	4 oz	—	—	1½ pt	—	6 oz	1 oz	—	1 pt
	5 oz	1½ pt	4 oz	—	—	1½ pt	—	5 oz	1 oz	—	1 pt
Th	6 oz	1½ pt	3 oz	4 oz	12 oz	—	—	6 oz	1 oz	1 pt	—
	5 oz	1½ pt	3 oz	4 oz	12 oz	—	—	5 oz	1 oz	1 pt	—
F	6 oz	1½ pt	4 oz	—	—	1½ pt	—	6 oz	1 oz	—	1 pt
	5 oz	1½ pt	4 oz	—	—	1½ pt	—	5 oz	1 oz	—	1 pt
S	6 oz	1½ pt	3 oz	—	—	—	14 oz	6 oz	1 oz	—	1 pt
	5 oz	1½ pt	3 oz	—	—	—	12 oz	5 oz	1 oz	—	1 pt

Menu B	Aged and Infirm. About 1 oz less meat
Menu C	Children 9-16 years. A little less meat
Menu D	Children 5-9 years. Less
Menu E	Children 2-5 years. Less still

Signed Frederick Gregson (Clerk)

Fig. 6a Menus for the Workhouse, 1843 and 1893

The Workhouse, the Almshouses and Other Charities 97

occasionally a little meat and some beer. The next year the Rochford Board of Guardians was set up to take charge of the poor of the whole Hundred, and at their first meeting in the *King's Head* on 12 October 1835,[13] T. Brewitt of Rayleigh was chairman, and Michael Comport, solicitor of Rochford, its first clerk. The workhouses at Canewdon and Hockley were then closed down and inmates transferred here.

Noble[14] said, 'off West Street to the north and a little distance from the Corn Exchange is the Union Workhouse built in 1837'. It had a fine open walk up to the house from Union Lane as it then began to be called. It was in March 1837[15] that Messrs. Steggle's tender for a house to cost £4,567 was accepted; the architect for the plans was Mr. Thorold of Norwich, but it cost £1,000 more by the time it was completed. It was built of yellow brick to hold some 300 inmates, but 250 seems to have been its biggest quota. It was partially opened on 1 November 1837[16] and in March 1838[17] two handmills were bought to be used for crushing bones for fertilisers. Colonel Kersteman and John Lodwick of Rochford Hall were present at the first board meeting when Rochford's representatives were Thomas Merrifield and George Wood. Mr. and Mrs. Claydon, who had been appointed on 24 December 1835[18] were then re-appointed master and matron of the Union, as it was named. White in 1848[19] said there were 181 inmates in July, whilst the *Essex Standard* for 1 January 1841 reported that the Union houses of Essex, including Rochford, received an extra allowance on Christmas day. Stone-breaking was introduced on 2 December 1873, and oakum-picking for men on 28 May 1889[20] with clothes-making for women. A little later net-making was brought in for both sexes, but the men also did any gardening or handiwork, and the women washed, cooked, sewed, and did any housework required.

The Union was indeed a dreadful place with its very strict rules of code and conduct, for on entry man and wife were separated, to meet very seldom, except at functions or Christmastide. The children fared little better, for they only came together for meals and schooling. The latter was undertaken in the precincts until Miss Tawke's intervention. The number of schoolmistresses who came and went yearly or oftener, despite double rations, was evidence of the spartan nature of the place. There were specific times for all things, including smoking, which was allowed but three times daily, 7.30 to 8.30, 12.30 to 1.30, and 5.30 to 6.30.[21] The inmates, children too, had to wear a large letter P stitched to their clothes, and penalties for infringement of the regulations were severe. For example, a small girl, Harriot Tibble, in 1840, was sentenced to a bread and water diet for a period, plus solitary confinement, whilst in September 1841 a boy was punished with an hour in a dark cupboard, which was well called the black hole, and, furthermore, was deprived of all companionship of the other children for a week. Comparison with the menu charts for the years 1843 and 1893 show a diet that was meagre and dull. It was soon after the first diet sheet was made, that a check of the cost of the paupers in the Union was put at 4d. per day; the date given as 10 October 1848.[22]

Under the provisions of the Local Government Act of 1929 the duties of governor were transferred to the county borough, so the last meeting of the guardians was held on 25 March 1930. A dinner at Garon's in Southend on 27 March that year signified the end of an era; the menu card included a picture of the entrance to the Union, with the building in the background.

The Workhouse, the Almshouses and Other Charities

Fig. 6b The Outer Cover of a Menu Card for a Dinner held to signify the end of the Board of Guardians, 1930

The Almshouses

At the far end of West Street are six tenements under one roof, a building of red brick, one storey high, with two gables to the front which project. They were mooted by Lord Rich in 1567, who intended them for the poor of the parish, but were not then erected, since the first Earl of Warwick, in his will dated 15 September 1617 said he had partly carried out his grandfather's wishes. This was because the £60 Rich was to have left was never entailed. He furthermore stated that two good loads of wood were to be delivered to the six poor folk from his woods at Rochford, with other small benefits. All this failed to come to pass, as I have instanced. Gradually, however, the almshouses took shape, and finally the building occupied some 3 roods 7 poles, with the large garden at the rear included, and a frontage of 105 feet. The owners of Rochford Hall have always kept the houses in repair, but the people were maintained by the parish, and in recent years much has fallen on the council, for alterations and additions have been made, As late as 1958, following an architect's report, they were modernised, and today have a comfortable sitting-room, some 16 feet by 10 feet, with a separate kitchen and bathroom. Part of the sitting-room is screened off to contain a single bed, with gas central heating recently installed. There were two reasons for the large number of alterations and repairs: firstly, no proper damp-course was ever put in, and, secondly, the brook often overflowed and spread across the road and front garden, so coming up to the brickwork. At one time the bottom half was re-bricked, but still damp showed, so eventually the upper half was done and completed with new guttering. This was in 1966, the cost on the first occasion was £3,000, and then £4,000 for the second attempt at a cure. Local appeals were launched, but only raised about one-tenth of this amount, so the council obtained a loan, as the Charity Commission said they were unable to foot the bill.

It was on 19 May 1922 that a deed of covenant was made with the Commission, who took over the charities as follows:

1. The charity called Lord Ryche's Almshouses;
2. That of Thomas Joslyn found by a will proved in the Prerogative Court of Canterbury on 12 December 1606;
3. The charity of an unknown donor for the use, benefit and advantage of the poor.

In the matter of the first charity the Rev. James Jeune Barnard, Rector of Rochford, Hugh Ranklin, miller, and Arthur Finnis Stilwell, gentleman, made the application, and Rev. Barnard made representation for the second and third charity. At the meeting held on 21 February 1922 and after notices had been affixed to the church door and the proposition advertised in the *Essex Weekly News* and *Essex Chronicle* of 7 April 1922, and despite William Gregson, solicitor of Southend, and Arthur Harrington, chemist of Southend, not agreeing in the first case, and likewise William Sorrell, ironmonger of Rochford, not in agreement in the case of the other two charities, the scheme was finally approved. There had been trustees appointed before this, for on 29 October 1869,[23] W. T. Meeson, Gregson and Harrington, and Alfred Rodd had been so appointed for the almshouse. The people for this charity were to be six aged poor, lame or impotent folk, of which one was to be an old woman, capable of looking after five men, keeping them in sickness and in health.

Lord Rich first specified they were to have 3s. 4d. per week, and 20s. 8d. at Christmas for a gown.

Other Charities

Thomas Joscelyn, in his will of 12 December 1604,[24] left 'Little Guards', sometimes called 'Snares', a house with land in Green Street, Hockley, for the relief of the poor.[25] The cottage was a boarded one, abutting on a road leading from Canewdon to Rayleigh on the north. The area of the land was given as approximately 15 acres, spread over three closes. In 1922 this was let to Alfred Hymas at a gross yearly rent of £24. On 6 August 1777 the property was given over to the overseers of Rochford.

The third charity was in three parts, consisting of land called 'Pest House' land, amounting to 9 acres, 3 roods, 9 poles or thereabouts, with a house from which the land took its name. In 1922 this was let to William Barnes for £20 annual rent. Also land in Ironwell Lane of 5 acres 4 poles extent let to Barnes for £6 rent. Here were two cottages facing south-east just beyond the bridge. They were boarded with attic bedrooms having dormer windows. In the right-hand one of the semi-detached pair lived Chapman, who was slightly deranged.[26] He would often show his feet through the window when lying in bed. The other house had many occupants, one named Gladwell. They were called the Poor Houses, and were once Hawkwell parish property. They were pulled down in 1960. Lastly, some 5,670 square feet of land in North Street, let to the Bishop brothers in 1922 for £10 annual rent.

Chapter Seventeen

TRANSPORT AND ROADS

Coaches

STAGE COACHES WERE FIRST written about in 1637 and by the middle of the century a fair number of towns were linked with such a service. By the year 1700 a national public system had appeared. Coach terminals were invariably at large inns in towns and villages, where food, shelter, accommodation and a change of horses could be had. In Essex, two such places were the *Rose and Crown* in Saffron Walden, and the *Blue Boar* at Maldon. In Rochford the two inns of the Market Square were the usual departure points. In 1761[1] a coach began from the *King's Head* and passed by way of Rayleigh and Billericay on to Shenfield, whilst in 1793[2] there was both a stage coach and a diligence that plied to London; the former from the *Rose and Crown*, North Street, on Monday, Wednesday and Friday at seven o'clock in summer and eight o'clock in winter. This went to the *Three Nuns*, Aldgate, and arrived at three o'clock in the afternoon, whilst the other left every Tuesday, Thursday and Saturday at 8 a.m. for the *Blue Boar*, Whitechapel. Since it arrived at 2 p.m., it was probably lighter and made fewer stops. Both returned at eight o'clock the next day and charged a fare of eight shillings.

In 1823 the 'Telegraph' left the Square for the *Bull*, Aldgate, daily at 8 a.m., with the 'Dispatch' from the *Vernon's Head* to the *Blue Boar*, Whitechapel, at the same time. J. Pease and Thomas Fitch were the respective proprietors of vans which also plied for hire then. In Dr. Asplin's diary (see Chapter 18) he made an entry on a journey he took on the 'Monitor' coach on 31 July 1826. He had come from South End, arrived in Rochford a little after four, breakfasted at Billericay and got to London at 9.40 a.m. He left again at three o'clock, and reached Prittlewell at 'three quarters before eight, a rate of 10 m.p.h.', he declared. The year 1832[5] saw the start of a different service, when Edward Minter began a run to and from Chelmsford, which his son, George, carried on from 1835-1839.[6]

The 'Dispatch' was still running in 1835, but began in South End before stopping at the *King's Head* for other passengers at 8.30 a.m. This was a daily service to Aldgate. Edward Brown[8] had joined the scene, for he took a van from his own house on Tuesdays and Fridays to the same destination, whilst Pease left the *Vernon's Head* half an hour previously for the *Boar's Head* on Monday and Thursday. G. Minter[9] meanwhile had reverted to the same days as Brown for his Chelmsford service. The Union (workhouse) minute book for 13 January 1841[10] said that Pease's van came from London in the afternoon, and recorded in October 1842 that the 'Telegraph' left the *Bull* at 2.30 p.m.

There must have been quite a demand thereafter from passengers, for in 1845[11] Thomas Beard, the blacksmith, had become a carrier for both people and parcels. He began his trip to Chelmsford from his works at the bottom of West Street and called at the Square. His vehicle replaced that of Minter, whilst three years later[12] Pease had been joined by his son, so henceforth the firm was known as J. and W. Pease, but the two still departed from the *Vernon's Head* on Monday, Thursday and Friday at 9 a.m. and returned on Tuesday and Friday at two o'clock, and

Transport and Coaches 105

on Saturday at 10.30 a.m. Beard continued until 1859[13] but in the meantime the ranks had been joined in 1849 by Robert Mountain, for he had a coach called the 'Rochford Union', which first went to and from Chelmsford. However, two years later[14] he altered his run and announced that on and after 31 March 1851 he would be leaving the *King's Head* at 7.30 on the mornings of Monday, Wednesday, Friday and Saturday for Brentwood, in time to catch the 1.30 p.m. train to London. He then waited until 4.30 p.m. for the express from the capital before he proceeded to Rochford, where he arrived at 7.45 in the evening. The fare for this journey was 5s. for a seat inside the coach, but only 3s. outside. It was in that same year that William Bishop, the draper, began a service to the *Three Nuns,* Aldgate, at first only on Monday, returning on Wednesday. Meanwhile the Pease firm had continued up to 1870[15] but in 1874[16] it was in T. Pease's name only, and thus it stayed until 1882.[17] Since Beard and Mountain had both concluded their service to Chelmsford it was taken over by James Higgleton, who went there and back from 1859 to 1867.[18]

Again in 1874[19] a fresh batch of names was found, including William Clark, who took over the Chelmsford circuit for at least four years.[20] There was also Henry Bloomfield, a well-known Rochford character, familiarly known as 'Tabby' because of the long fur-lined hat he wore which had earpieces. He started his journey to Southend from his house, No. 4, on the south side of Weir Pond Road. He kept two donkeys in a shed where the present pair of brick houses are further down on the same side, which are today numbered 18 and twenty. The initials W.F.S. are over the space between the two doorways as they were built by William Smoothy, who had the ironworks just beyond them. Bloomfield used the donkeys to pull a shay for passenger traffic, but he also took round faggots called 'bavins' for sale. Again J. Brown and T. Scott appeared for the first time in that year, the former going to and from Southend railway station, the latter to Wakering and Prittlewell and both carried on until 1882.[21] It was in that year that T. Bush left the *King's Head* at 7 a.m. for Chelmsford to return at three o'clock. A newcomer on the scene of travel was the conveyance which left Creeksea Ferry, calling at the *New Ship* en route to the railway terminus at Southend. Although it was found for the first time as in 1882, I was told it had run for some years before that.

Then a lull ensued for a few years, when again in 1890 there came several new names. First amongst them was Daniel Harvey who was the licensee of the *Prince of Wales* in North Street. He had quite a conveyancing business as well, for when on 6 June 1895[22] his stock was sold, there were seven horses, two ponies, two broughams, and two carts left after some others had been sold. He made a great point of starting on time at 8 a.m. for his trade to Southend and back. William Hornsby only began in 1914 when he lived with his family on the south side of West Street, almost opposite 'The Hollies', the house now numbered fifty-seven. He was generally called 'Buck', and had his sons, Mike and Bill, help him in the trade. One married and lived next door to his father. They had stables, off Union Lane, but behind the row of houses there, and they used the pump lower down the street by the brook, to clean and wash horses and carts. Yet, despite the railway and motors, a diligence still ran thrice weekly to Aldgate in 1916.[23]

The Coming of the Railway

The railway came to Rochford on 3 October 1889, with much pomp and ceremony. Miss Tawke (see Chapter 22) in her *Recollections* said that the first train left Southend at 7.13 a.m. and carried 92 people, of whom 37 booked to Rochford, at which station Hunt, the church clerk, was seen on the platform. Arthur Harrington had secured the first ticket, but others on the train included Superintendent Hawtree of the Essex police with his wife, H. Harper, the Rochford draper, and T. Quy, junior, the ironmonger. Some of the adults were given a free ride to Wickford station and back, and the children meanwhile were entertained to tea in the company's goods shed.

F. W. Francis, the printer's son, gave another account on the occasion of his golden wedding in July 1931, for he declared that H. A. Rumsey, the auctioneer, and himself were joint secretaries of the local committee formed to grace the occasion, and that later the chairman, Major Tawke of 'The Lawn', presented each of them with a testimonial so well did the celebrations go. 'Quite an event', he said. William Reeve was the first stationmaster until 1899, then came J. H. Glasscock, who had a long stay here until he retired in 1927. Several others were here for short periods, but A. F. Smith stayed from 1932 to 1954, F. Winchester (1944-9), Cyril W. Tunn (1949-54), and, finally, F. G. Turner (1954-65)[24] since which date there has been one stationmaster for several local stops.

Travel by Water
Transport of goods by water was never a great problem in Essex, where many parts of the coast were cut by small rivers and streams and where tidal estuaries penetrated deep into the heart of the county. Such were the Colne and Roman rivers, the Pont and its tributary the Brain, forming to join the Blackwater, the Chelmer, with its helpers, the Can and Wid, and, finally, the Crouch, which is

Rochford's closet river-link, save for its own smaller stretch of water, the Roche. In early days the upper reaches of all these rivers were kept clean and clear both by man and also by the very frequent movement of boats, particularly the barge traffic so prevalent around this area, indeed, for the whole of East Anglia. The smaller streams, too, figured in this frequentation, though not always on lawful business since their presence was a great aid to smuggling, a business in which Essex men were second to none.

Broomhills, a farm with a mill so close to Rochford as almost to be a far-flung wharf, had its own quay and was served by at least its own two corn sloops, which made weekly deliveries to London markets. W. T. Meeson and A. M. and H. Rankin shared in this trade in later years, from 1851 to 1900, but which had begun many years before that, under the banner of W. Rankin, when trips were made to St. Catherine's dock in 1839, and earlier still for J. Barnes in 1823-32.

Roads and the Turnpike

Parishes were made officially responsible for the repair of roads in 1555. Then a system of compulsory labour of six days a year by each parishioner was set up, supervised a little later by justices at special highway sessions through two surveyors appointed annually for each district. There were important exceptions to this rule of parochial responsibility; certain streets in towns could be left to paving commissions under local bye-laws, and turnpike roads were to be repaired by their own trustees under private acts. These trusts spread greatly after the Jacobite rebellion of 1715 showed the need for more and better roads. The first Turnpike Act was in 1663. Between 1770 and 1790

Transport and Coaches

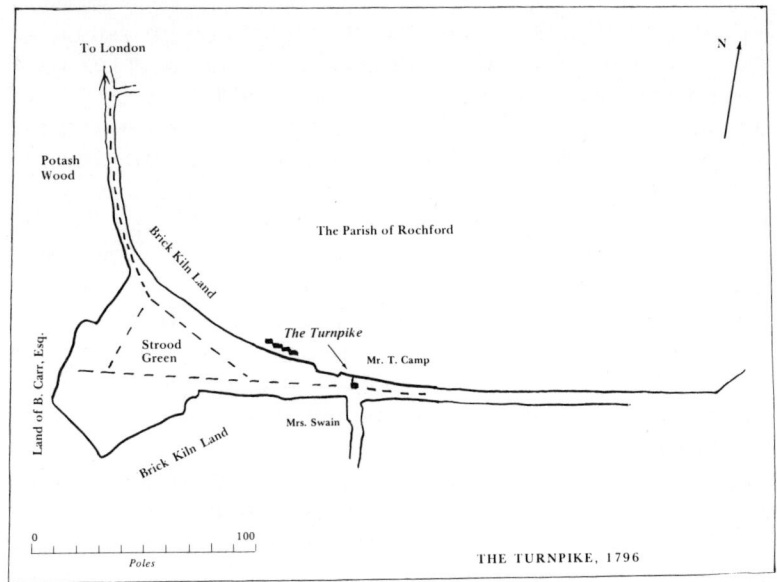

Fig. 7a The Rochford Turnpike, 1796

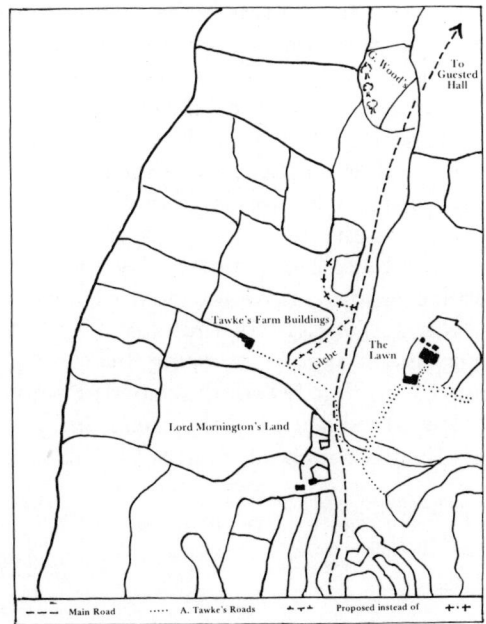

Fig. 7b Road to Rochford Glebe, The Lawn and Guested Hall, from Tithe Map, 1862

an additional 600 Trusts[25] were set up, as private companies gained Acts of Parliament enabling them to close certain roadways with gates. Tolls could thus be levied on all users except for post horses and certain coaches carrying mail.[26] The tolls were often farmed out to lessees which made for increased charges and less supervision and hence, poorer upkeep. We are told that Telford himself designed toll-houses, milestones, and even wood and iron gates to assist the spread.

Despite this, many roads were in a sorry state even in the early 19th century, so that the proprietors of stage coaches and the like, qualified their timings with the phrase, 'If God permits'.[27] Some of the roads in and around Rochford 'were in a state of nature', said Benton[28] who went on to say that farmers objected to them being improved, believing it would increase the rent. It was comforting to find, therefore, that Young declared, 'it is impossible to say too much in praise of the roads of most districts of Essex',[29] but Benton was not in full accord with this, for he continued by saying that drunks took the middle of the road when riding home, 'since the splashes of their horse's feet assured them of safety'. Great Wakering had its streets ploughed and roads were levelled with harrows both here and in Thundersley, Benton said, 'and as for the town of Rochford, the roadway was frightful with footpaths protected from vehicles by huge posts'.[30] Cannon were used in the town such as the one I have spoken of in Old Ship Lane, and another by the side of what was the old police station, now the post office, in North Street. This last was set upright in the corner of the building to off-set carts and waggons carrying beasts for slaughter down the lane. Cook[31] in 1807 described a journey from Cambridge to Rochford with another beginning at Rochford, crossing the River Crouch at South Fambridge,

Transport and Coaches

where there was a ferry, and on to Braintree. Mogg in 1822[32] gave a similar description, though he was merely updating the records of Lieut.-Colonel Paterson, who had written some 40 years previously. He instances the same river crossing, but added, 'the road then came to Rochford by way of Ashingdon'.

Reverting to the turnpikes, one was placed on the outskirts of Rochford on the Hall Road, and another was further south. Chapman and Andre's map of 1777 shows the former as opposite the entrance to Cherry Orchard Lane. The Record Office have a statement of receipts of the First District of Essex Turnpike Trusts; the amount for the period June to November 1866[33] was £2,028 4s. 11d. Statement No. 2, for the time between 31 October and 31 December 1866, records the sale of the Rochford Turnpike for £118 10s. 0d.[34] Gratuities were then paid to the toll collectors, 20 in all, who shared £135 between them, with a further sum of £311 to be distributed amongst the parishes of the six sectors of District One. It was just prior to this that Mr. Codd had repaired the Rochford bridge on 5 October 1864.[35] A gentleman who re-visited Southend in 1794[36] said, 'the two Turnpike roads, one through Rochford and the other one nearer the coast . . . had been much improved'. This was a reference to the road from Shenfield through to Rayleigh, where it divided, one part carrying on to Rochford via Hockley, the other proceeding to Southend.

The coming of the railways did the same for the turnpikes as it had done for the stage coaches and other forms of road conveyance. So much so that the toll bar at Irlan, between Manchester and Liverpool, which was let in 1830 for £1,300 per annum could not be sold the following year for £500.[37]

The Turnpike Cottage

This, an old wooden cottage, set on the grass verge of Hall Road and fronting it to face Cherry Orchard Lane, could very well have been the one indicated on the 1777 map, for a gate across the road here would have caught the traffic entering the town on the main road. I was told the toll was 2d. for a cart, and 1d. for a pedestrian, but cannot substantiate this. The cottage had four rooms, two up and two down, but water was obtained from Pelham's farm next to it. It was pulled down in May 1964 by order of Mr. Tabor.

The first inmates I found listed were the Marvins in 1889; the wife sold home-made sweets, the husband worked at the farm. Then followed the Haggars, and David Bines after them, but by 1916 K. H. Barkham was given. A widow, Mrs. Gentry, had it from 1919 to 1931. Then, George Frederick Marles until 1941, when Frederick George Everett had it nine years. G. Bond came next, with Mr. Kupke in his turn. Finally Ernest G. Coleman came in 1959 to 1 April 1963, dying there. Most of these early inhabitants worked at 'The Lawn' for Major Tawke, or later for Mr. Tabor. It is thought to have ceased its former use well before 1866. A possible clue to this was the path which started on the road higher up, near the bend and opposite Ark Lane. This track skirted the road, running almost parallel to it, and came out on to Hall Road just before the bridge. By this means tolls were evaded by most users except for large carts. A Court Roll of the Manor of Rochford, undated, gave Arthur Tawke of 'The Lawn', 'as holden of a messuage, formerly Turnpike house . . . Turnpike since removed in or upon Stroud Green'.[38] It seems probable that the turnpike was strung across the road later, prior to the bend, to deter people from taking the untaxed path.

1. The Market Hall, Rochford

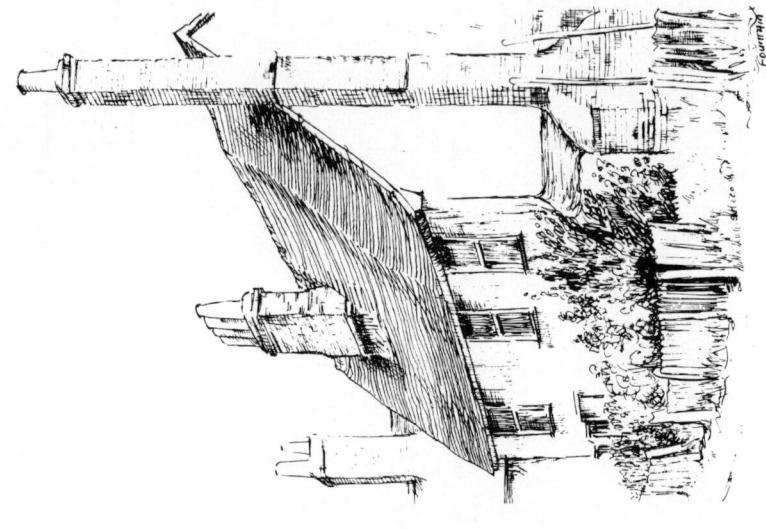

3. The Malting Cottages, Weir Pond Road, Rochford

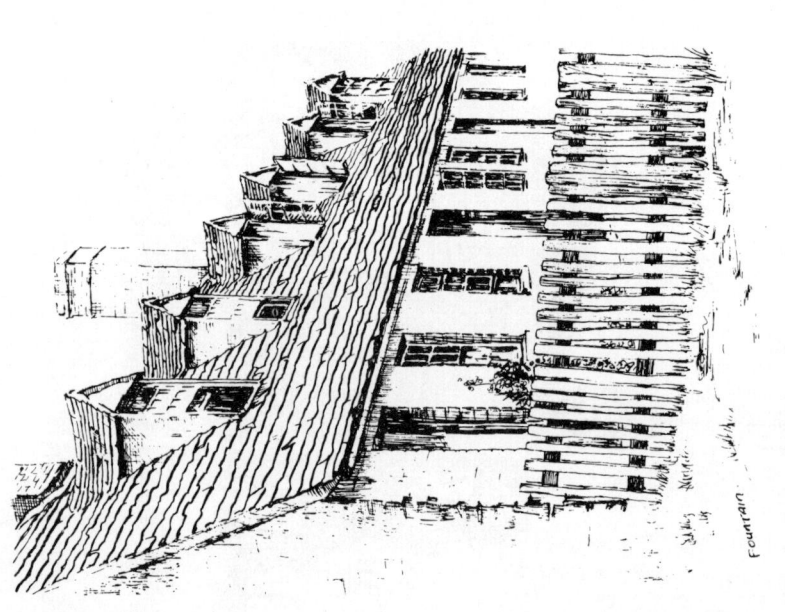

2. The Cottages, Union Lane, Rochford

4. The Market Square, Rochford

5. Front View of Rochford Hall

6. Back View of Rochford Hall

7. One of the Octagonal Towers of Rochford Hall

8. The Old Barn, Doggett's Farm, Rochford

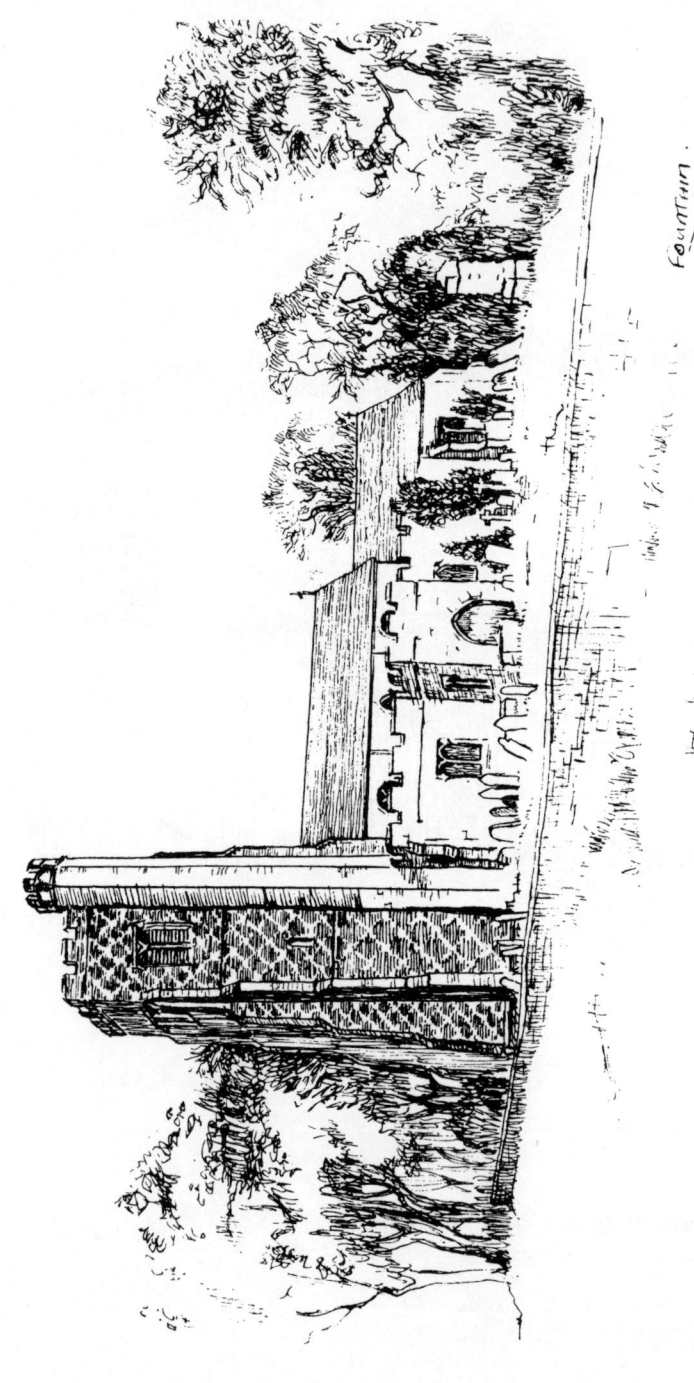

9. The Church, Hall Road, Rochford

10. The Nine Bay Barn, Great Doggett's, Rochford

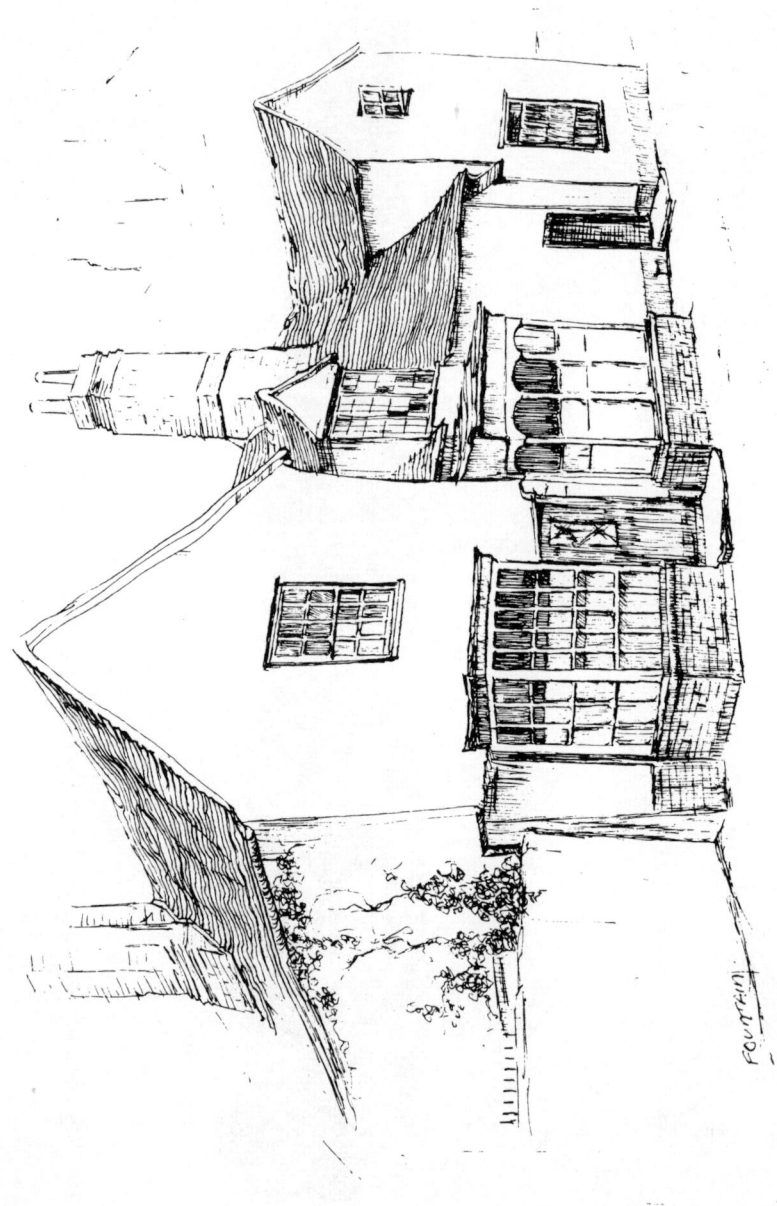

11. The Old Moot House, 17 South Street, Rochford.

12. Sydenham House School, South Street, Rochford

13. The Old Mill House, West Street, Rochford

14. The site of the *Horse and Groom* inn, Southend Road

Chapter Eighteen

SOME ROCHFORD PERSONALITIES AND FAMILIES

WILLIAM TAYLOR MEESON was born in 1821 and died on 7 April 1914 at the age of ninety-three. In his lifetime he owned a large part of Rochford, particularly round Ashingdon Road. He was a well-known figure in the district and in London, for he made weekly trips to the City every Monday morning, when he was driven to the railway station in a wheeled trap, wearing his customary top hat. He was a very strict man and was alleged to have driven across a field of growing crops to check on his workmen. He always carried a walking cane, some four feet long, and locals claimed this as the reason for his upright carriage. He married one of the Merryfield sisters, their fathers having been the owner of Doggetts until his death in 1847. He enclosed part of Swaine's field, called the 'Priest's House' now, which he let to the council for a hospital. The fence would help to keep in the germs, it was said. He farmed Great Doggetts, which he bought in 1867[1] along with a deal of other property.

He used the corner shop in the Market Square, opposite the bank, as an agricultural and machine shop. Some of the vehicles were stored here, the rest in the stables of the *King's Head* in Back Lane. These he sold, on market day, to neighbouring farmers. He had six sons, Arthur, Claypole, Merrifield, Henry, Humbert, and Frank. The latter lived in 'Swaine's House', with his two sisters after his father's death.

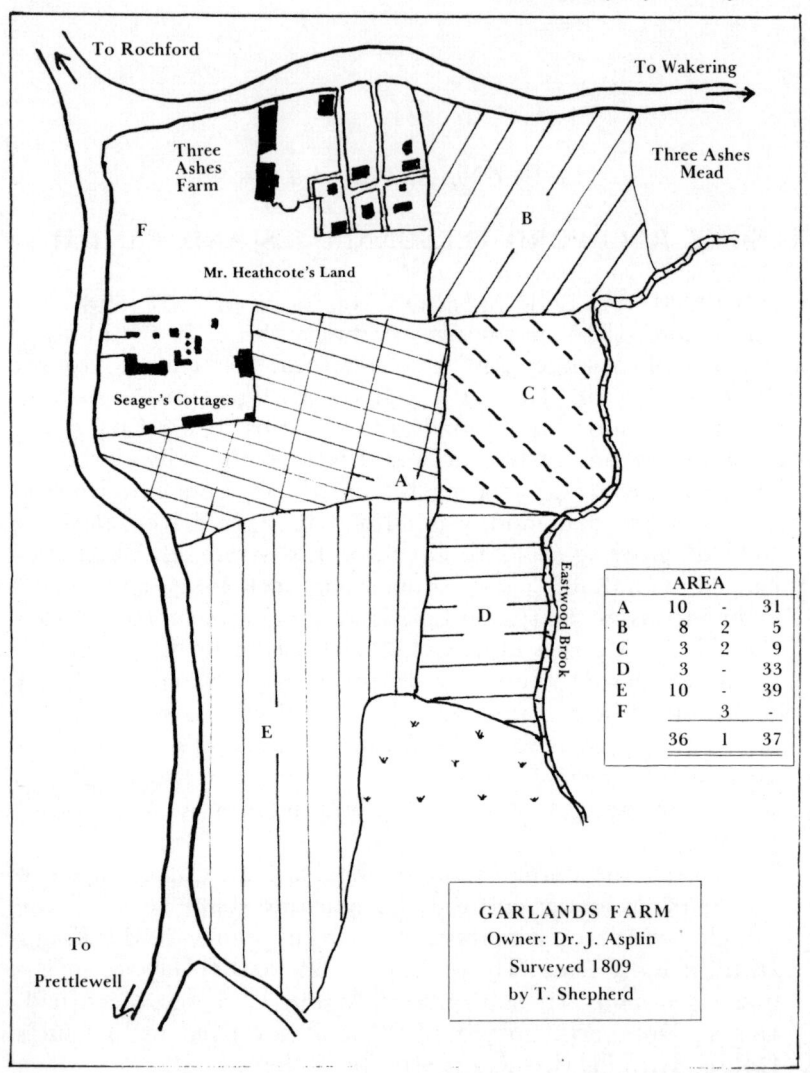

Fig. 8

Some Rochford Personalities and Families 115

Dr. Asplin

In the library at Colchester there is a handwritten diary of Dr. Asplin. Unfortunately, it only covers the years 1825-28, but it records among other facts, that on 18 February 1825 Sparrow and Company's bank (Rochford) suspended payment. There was a copy of a map in the drawers of the reference library, Southend, showing him as having a farm called Garlands, when it was surveyed in 1809. The Three Ashes farm is also named on it, with Mr. Heathcote in residence. The Asplin family lived at Little Wakering Hall, for a Jonas Asplin, possibly the doctor's father, died there in 1774, and a Francis Asplin in 1799, but he himself lived for some years, 1826-35, opposite St. Mary's church, Prittlewell. He reported the trial of Long Pole Wellesley of Rochford Hall on 3 November 1826, when damages were awarded to Captain Bligh because of adultery with his wife. He had connections with the family of Stephen Jackson of Doggett's farm. He mentioned in his daily record the names of Kersteman from Wakering, Vanderzee, the Rochford solicitor, Vanderwood, a Southend merchant, Scratton of the Priory, Tabor of 'The Lawn' and Hall, and Comport, another Rochford attorney. He was a noted character in Southend as well as here, where he had a surgery, for he wrote:[2] 'visited Harvey the baker at Rochford, with others to see me at Gullocks'. It was thought this was a reference to the watchmaker. He also held on lease the corner house in the Square, lately Shelley's, the grocer, and today a supermarket called Lipton.

Francis, the Printer

William Francis, who was born in Ruckings, near Ashford, Kent, married Anna Waghorn on 18 February 1781.[3] Before her death in 1851[4] they had nine children, with William as the eldest son, although the second child. He also had a large family of at least 16 children, of whom Jabez came 15th and Joseph last. It was Jabez who came to Rochford on 23 July 1852 as foreman of the printing works which W. H. Jackson, the auctioneer-cum-ironmonger, had purchased in 1840 at Romford, and which had been set up in West Street. When Rodd, who had taken over the printing works, died suddenly in 1863, Jabez borrowed some money to buy the business. He had by that time sent for his wife and children, who came by train to Brentwood, where Pease, the carrier, who had already brought over their furniture, met them in his coach. After a year the works were moved to the south side, where he had a house. Clever with his hands, Jabez made picture frames, took photographs, played the glasses and used a magic lantern to give lectures. Being very musical he was commissioned to buy a harmonium for the Congregational church, and after travelling to London where he purchased an instrument for £30, he was appointed honorary organist, as he was the only one able to play it. A branch shop was opened in 1872 over the auction rooms in Southend, where William, his son, who had served his apprenticeship in London, became manager. About this time he enlarged the West Street premises by taking over the adjoining shop to use as a stationers. This had been the old bank house, with Giles the manager, but had been moved to larger premises higher up the street. He had turned his hand to making small iron presses with similarly-made type, but was forced to stop when others copied his ideas in wood. Many pictures exist of the old Market Hall and other buildings, the result of his work which he combined with portraits to bring him in a little extra cash. The *Southend Telephone*, with the first edition printed on Friday, 28 May 1880, was begun by him. It carried advertisements for H. Harper, clothier and hatter, H. Simms, grocer, the engineering firm of Carey, Stilwell and Birch, and for W. Bishop, the draper. Jabez, who had 12 children, had his story published in 1916,[5] and his son, W. J., in 1926.[6] Another son, Frederick Walter, became postmaster for the town.

John Clarkson
He lived in North Street, opposite Old Ship Lane, where he carried on his trade of chimney sweep. He proved to have had a good education, for once, after scalding himself, found he was in hospital where he astonished the staff with his knowledge. A tall, gaunt man, six feet in height, he always dressed in a long black coat, well kept, although his other garments were shabby. He called himself the prodigal son, which may have been a clue to his learning, and some claimed he was a clergyman's son. He charged 4d. to sweep a chimney, 'pulling a wooden box on wheels round to his calls', with his brushes and sack inside. He was a keen photographer, for on fine days, especially in summer, he would walk to the pier at Southend, and there hire out his telescope at 1d. a time. For this exploit he was often nicknamed 'Johnny, Johnny, shoot the stars'. Outside his house he hung up a large boot as a sign that he also did some cobbling.

The Bishops
William Bishop was born in 1839, and died on 1 February 1904. By his wife, Elizah, who died on 8 January 1892, he had a large family. He began as a marine store dealer in North Street, the premises now used by Bacon as a smithy, opposite Weir Pond Road. His eldest son, also called William, was the draper who began the business at the corner of South Street and West Street. He also used

Holt Farm on Ashingdon Road where he kept horses and carts which were used in his trade. Fred was the second son, who married Ann Francis. Arthur was the third son, who later set up trading as an ironmonger on the north side of the Square after a quarrel with his father. Next in line was Albert, the fourth son, who was the journeyman for the family and who married Nora Richmond, a sister of Florence, who had married Arthur. Stanley came next, and he opened a furniture shop in Back Lane just beside the bakery. There was a yellow stone dated 1876 in the far end of this tall building. Lavinia, next in line, helped in the china store her father had promoted. This was in the shop, early known as Kernot, the druggists. then more lately as the Delph tea house, and today the Conservative club, situated a little further down West Street than her father's shop. Mary Ann often called Polly, the next daughter, helped all round, whilst Jenny, the last of the children, married Palmer, the butcher. William, the father, bought the Wesleyan building in North Street in 1822 and had it converted into three two-storey cottages, and the vestry altered to make a club house for his sons and daughters and their friends. A narrow side passage led to the club by the side of the end cottage and was called Old Chapel Yard. The whole was later purchased by the hospital to make a new entrance.

The Priors

These were well-known Rochford folk, the father being the landlord of the *New Ship* for a number of years from 1868 to 1888. This was Henry, spoken of in the chapter on King's Hill and the Lawless Court. The son, Punch, had a wooden house built in 1885 in East Street, almost opposite the inn and his father. Today it is a tobacconist and hairdressing establishment, but he used it as a furniture shop and displayed some of his goods from an overhanging balcony on the second floor. It was afterwards used for the same purpose by E. Doe. The son had another wooden house built, on the same side of the street, which he called 'Ivanhoe'. It was some distance away, up the street, and was pulled down fairly recently when a new-type brick house took its place.

The Gregsons

William Gregson was born in Rochford on 28 April 1842 and died in Southend in 1926, after becoming Southend's first town clerk. He was the second son of William Gregson of 'The Cottage', Stroud Green, which was demolished in 1921. He began his career in the firm of Comport, the Rochford solicitor, becoming a partner later on, by which time he had married Mary E. Jackson. It is believed he had 'Fir Tree House' in the early days after his marriage. They had a son, Harold, born in 1870, who died in March 1895, and was buried in the churchyard here. Frederick was the first son, and he, too, became a solicitor. At first he lived in 'The Lavenders', West Street, but then moved to 'Connaught House' in the Square. He was the clerk to the Rochford guardians for many years.

Arthur Harrington

He was a chemist in West Street for nigh on 40 years from 1853 to 1891. The premises has kept that trade ever since, and today the Co-operative Society have modernised the building but retained its business. It is still a three-storey house, which, when Farrington first came, was built mainly of lath and plaster. Soon after, like many others in the town, it underwent the fashionable change and was largely replaced with bricks. When I first went to Rochford in 1957 there were five bricks with the date 1862 on, and at least two had the initials of the bricklayers. When it was re-fronted in 1970 four were cemented over, but one was left showing. I saw one of Harrington's original recipe books, dated 1884, when I spoke to the chemist there in 1970. The building had large cellars. It was here the mineral-water business began about 1856. Several boys were kept to bottle and cork the various flavours and stone bottles with strings to keep the corks in were first used before a new idea was brought in, using a marble in the end, which released the drink and the fizz, when it was pushed in. For a number of years the cost was 1d. a bottle. Even today, one of the hooped ladders used to slide the four and a half gallon casks called pins down into the cellar, survives. The third floor had a number of small rooms which together with the presence of a bell system led to the belief that they had been servants' quarters. It was a very large house at one time and had its own well which was afterwards cemented over, but directions as to its whereabouts were painted on the wall, on the side furthest away. This was in the garden, and I was told when I inquired a year or so before my later search, that a different coloured grass grew over that spot.

William Pearce Kernott

His name, spelt sometimes with one T, has cropped up several times before. He was born in 1797 and came to Rochford when he was 40 years old, and purchased the premises of H. Thorne on 29 October 1839 for £715. This was the shop he made a druggists, facing on to the Square. The purchase was made at the *King's Head* next door, with William Quy, the ironmonger, acting as auctioneer. It had four bow-fronted windows, two up, two down, which came out on to the path. The door to the shop was between the lower pair when its frontage was 26 feet. I was told he built a connecting passage from his back bedroom, out over Back Lane to join up to his coach-house on the other side. It sounded feasible and was described to me by P. Roughton, who had the business opposite. The front premises, the chemist's shop and house were later purchased by W. Bishop on 24 October 1903 and opened by him as a china department. Kernott died on 6 July 1842, leaving the premises to Lavinia his wife, who survived him a number of years. His son, Charles, emigrated to Geelong in Victoria, Australia, where he died on 26 March 1882. A member of the family named White, who lived close to Charles called his house, at Bream Creek, 'Rochford Hall'.

Moss, father and son

The father, William, began the hairdressing firm next door to where Kernott had his shop. He was recorded as early as 1845, and then was joined by his son in 1865, but Francis's name appeared alone from 1874 and continued up to 1916.

The son was a very noted character, as was his father. Francis kept a diary of the daily events of Rochford and its folk which he meticulously maintained. It must have contained a wealth of stories, for he was a man of great integrity who was often called in as an arbiter to settle disputes, where his word was accepted as law. These secrets he well kept, and I regretted I was unable to find the record. He was a tall, well-built man who sported a good black beard and was always well dressed. He was the Union barber for many years and it was reported he often did his trade there for little or nothing. Cockerton, a farmer from Barling, who had another farm in Sutton, was one of the son's most eccentric customers, for he would not enter the shop, but would have his hair cut or be shaved seated in his ponytrap in the middle of the Square. Moss walked to Colchester to see the damage caused by the earthquake of 22 April 1884, and the trip did not cause him any concern since he used to go on foot to his shop at Leigh twice a week, on Tuesdays and Fridays, returning by the same means. His wife and daughter rented the shop in an opposite corner of the Square, which had been the *Star* inn, but had ceased in 1884, and here they conducted a newspaper and stationery store.

Chapter Nineteen

THE FARMS

MANY OF THE FARMS in and around the town were part of the homage of the court of Rochford Hall. The great sale of 1867 of this manor estate alone contained over 30 lots, the money realised was over £80,000, without lettings, and four major farms, some smaller ones and other properties were included.

Rochford Hall Farm

In the chapter on the Hall much has been written about the farm. When Sir James Tylney Long's property was surveyed in 1791[1] the farm was given as having occupied 589 acres 1 rood 24 poles, which was as much as all the other farms and property owned as part of the Rochford estate. From early days all these were part of the homage of the Manor Court of Rochford Hall, although Muilman said Doggetts itself was a reputed manor with Coombes, but he was the only one giving such a guide. When the Rochford estate was sold in 1867 there were some 37 lots up for sale (see General map, key plan, p. 124). Between the Hall and the farm there was a good orchard and just beyond the church was the Wilderness.[2] This was once a beautiful retreat, said Benton, well stocked with noble thorn bushes, which featured in the murder of Mrs. Emma Hunt (see chapter on the Police). Although many of its tenant farmers did little more than the bare minimum, there

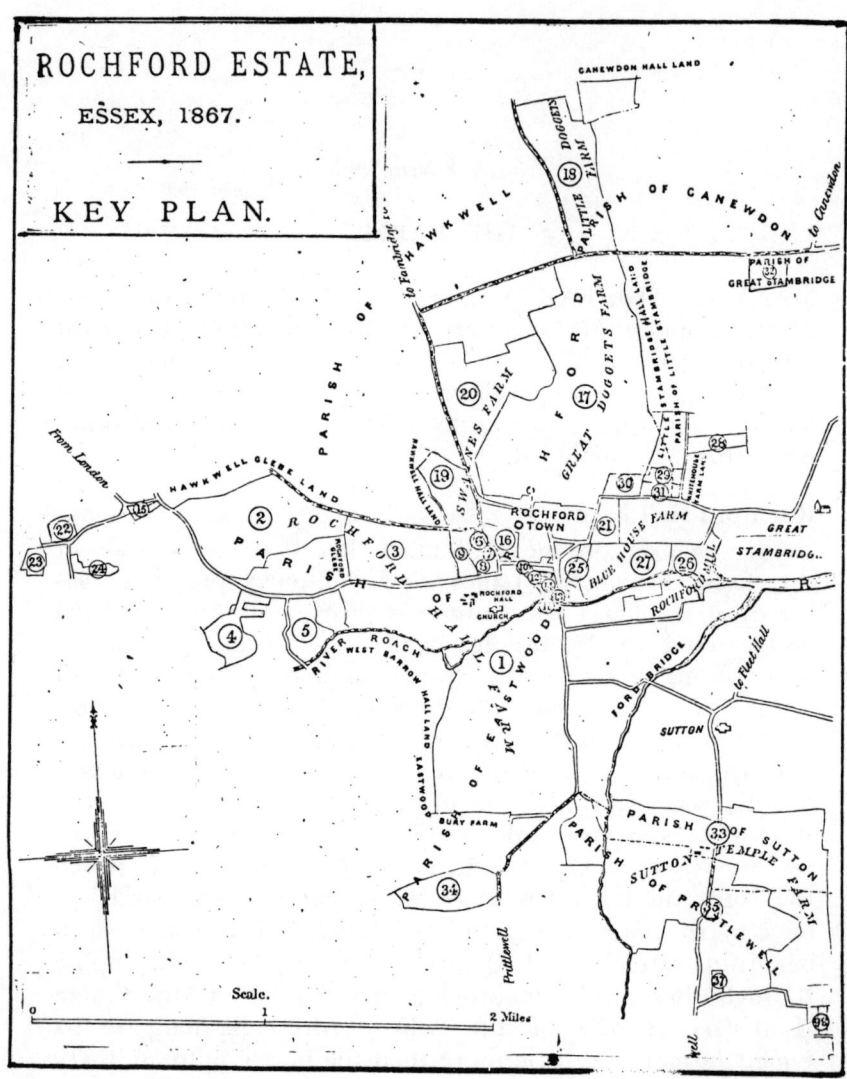

Fig. 9

The Farms

were some who ventured from a narrow agricultural path. The Hall farm became a recognised place for the cultivation of mustard. Harry Chapmen took me to the spot where the cottage that his father had lived in had stood, when he worked on the estate. Just beyond was a large shed with open rafters on which the 10 to 12 sledges used in hauling the mustard were kept.

J. R. Smith[3] in his book on the Tylney Long estates, said the rent of the farm was £848 per annum.

Lessees of Rochford Hall Farm

Earl Tylney to—
> Thomas Ffirman in 1688;
> Robert Tilden in 1698 for 21 years;
> —. Richardson in 1705 for 21 years;
> William Barnard in 1727;
> Thomas Burdor in 1731. It then contained 581 acres;
> Thomas Spurgeon in 1740;
> William Barnard in 1746;

Leased by Sir James Tylney-Long, who died in 1794 to—
> William Weld in 1762 for 21 years;
> Cannon Barrington in 1767 (part lease);
> James Wright in 1773, with part leased to John Wade, 1772;
> John Chapman 1776–1797;
> George Wright 1800–1810. Rent £700 p.a.

His son, same name, died 1805, to—
> Various tenants.

Catherine Tylney Long, 1825, to—
> John Lodwick, 24 December 1840. Still here in 1845.

Great Doggett's Farm

This was probably the next in order of importance as a part of the large estate. The figures again from 1796[4] were 366 acres 2 roods 15 poles. In 1305 Robert and Alice Dogett held a messuage here and 26 acres of arable land,[5] purchased by Beatrix Dogett, and 60 acres purchased by John Rocheford, 'holden of the King as the Honor of Reylie'; John of that family held it in 1338, followed by William. Then followed a long gap for the next occupier traced was Edward Rawlyn in 1577, but his name appeared with William Paynter and John Freebarn, so perhaps it was part-leased. It was then let at £20 13s. 4d. p.a.

It was situated principally in Rochford and extended from Brays Lane across in a southerly direction to Potash Lane, now called Daly's Road, but its western boundary extended across to part of Swaine's farm, which itself carried on across to Ashingdon Road. A part of the farm continued on the other side of Brays Lane and was generally called Little Doggetts, being thus situated in the parish of Canewdon. Benton who wrote about it declared it an excellent residence with extensive gardens and five cottages. Four of these, two semi-detached and two singles, were on the private road from Brays Lane going south to the house, the other near the Bobbing ponds, which was of wooden construction. One notable occupier was Stephen Jackson, who died 24 December 1706[6] after being the high constable of the Rochford Hundred. He was a relative of the Asplin family. W. H. Meeson purchased it in 1867 for £18,100, when it contained 349 acres.[7] He presented a plan to the Essex Record Office dated 1881, which showed the five cottages still intact. He remained here until his death in 1914, then in March 1917 the farm was purchased by the Squier family, who are still in occupation.

The Farms

Lessees of the Farm

Lord Castlemain to—
Thomas Spurgeon 1712-1733 and 1738-1756.

Earl Tylney to—
John Spurgeon, his son 1756-1777;
Cannon Barrington 1777-1784;
Daniel Dale 1784-1805. The rent £75 p.a.

Lady Catherine Tylney Long to—
John Barrington 1802-1810. Rent £420 p.a.;
J. Barrington 1823-1822. Rent £630 p.a.;
J. Barrington 1823-1828;
Thomas Merrifield held it in 1844. He died 15 March 1847.

Swaine's Farm

This name was spelt many ways: Sweyn, Swayn, Sweyne, Swayne, Swaines, but all, perhaps, came from the name Suene spoken of in the first chapter. It, too, was part of the honour court of Rochford Hall, when as part of the estate of Tylney Long it was situated on both sides of the Ashingdon Road with the house on the west side. It was this side that had the smaller area of 33 acres 2 roods. The house then had an upper floor for servants, a first floor with two bedrooms, two dressing rooms, and a lumber room and a ground floor with entrance hall, drawing room, dining room, kitchen, store room, cellar, etc., with a brewhouse and garden and outside farm buildings with meadowland. It was then let to James Cockerton, who bought it for £2,905.[9] The next lot, No. 20, the other part of the farm on the east side of the road, carried on until joined up with Doggett's. It contained 98 acres 2 roods 26 poles. Part one was separated from the Rochford Hall farm by Ironwell Lane. Although this part, too, was let to Cockerton, Meeson bought it in 1867 for £5,000[10] and later paid the same amount for the remainder. An early occupant was Henry Colefax, who in 1577[11] was paying rent at £5 10s. p.a., when the Earl of Warwick was lord of the manor.

Lessees
Earl Tylney to—
John Fortescue 1704-1709;
John Dale 1756-1784;
Ralph Silversides, born 1783, died 1843.

Catherine Tylney Long to—
Robert Harrison 1805-1910. Rent then £150 p.a.

Earl of Mornington to—
James Samuel Cockerton 1858-1861. Rent £255 p.a.
J. S. Cockerton 1861-1867

Coombe's Farm

This farm was sometimes called the Blue House Farm[12] and although much of it was in the parish of Rochford it extended into both Stambridge parishes. It was situated on the road leading from the east side of the town to Great Stambridge and was joined on its north-west side to Doggetts. It extended on its south side to the river which separated it from Eastwood. In earlier days it was a moated manor,[13] with a tenant named Mary Carey, daughter of Sir Thomas Bullen. By 1577 it was in the tenure of Edward Grantham at a rent of £10 2s. 8d. It was sold by the Earl of Mornington to John Offord of the *King's Head* inn for £7,000, in four separate lots, when the total area was 136 acres, and again this was part of the 1867 sale. A further portion, some eight acres of the farm, which had been let to William Daniel was granted to him on lease at £32 3s. 6d. per annum, for use as a brickfield.

Great Bray's Farm

This was down the lane with the same name, off Ashingdon Road, and once extended into Ashingdon itself and across into Hawkwell, but the residence was in Rochford. Previous to 1819 it belonged to Thomas Keyes and others, for in that year it was sold to Daniel Shirley of Barking, in whose family it remained until bought on 22 October 1834[14] by William Prevost of Middlesex, who died 29 September 1836. It was sold on 6 May 1870 for £3,900 to W. T. Meeson.[15] When R. G. Bates had it in 1922, it was a wooden house with thatched roof with a large pond slightly to its right. It remained so until its present owner, Mr. Bull, pulled it down in 1946, and in its place built a brick and tile house. He showed me a notice board, found in the old barn by the entrance gate, which was the property of Meeson and was exhibited to warn people that a £1 fine was the liability for damage to trees, fences or hedges belonging to him. The 1870 sale took place at the Mart, Tokenhouse Yard, London, when the property comprised the farmhouse and garden, a cottage, and various outbuildings, with an area of just over 78 acres.

Evan's Farm

Benton gave Stroud Green as the site of this place. The Green was once the name for that part of Hall Road beyond Ark Lane, but its meaning was never clear. A better description would be to say the farm had an entrance off Cherry Orchard Lane, although the house itself faced on to Hall Road. It was oft-times called 'Parries' for no apparent reason and was held in 1773 by Thomas Sly then by Mary Swaines in 1779. In 1800[16] G. D. Carr had it as a copy holder of Rochford Manor. John Pole and Robert Evans[17] were next here, followed by Michael Compart, solicitor, who held it on 24 October 1820. It was in Mary Wynne's name in 1840, followed by Philip Hicks in 1849, with J. T. Chapman of the *King's Head* inn, who bought it in 1865,[18] then W. H. Rankin took it over in 1858/9. It was sold on Thurdsay, 9 September 1886[19] when its contents were listed as 'house with barn, stables and chaisehouse, sheds and yards, with a good garden to the house and 11 acres of arable land close to the proposed station on the Great Eastern railway extension now being made from Brentwood to Southend'. The house had two front parlours, kitchen, scullery and pantry on the ground floor with four bedrooms above, with dormer windows. G. B. Hilliard was the auctioneer when the estate was disposed of at the *Old Ship*. H. Blakely held it from 1907 to 1916, followed by J. McConnell before it returned to the Blakely family.

Golden Cross Farm

Boswell Avenue, off the east side of Ashington Road has been recently built. Its north side would have been the boundary of this farm, which went on towards Ashingdon. It was held in 1835 by W. J. Cockerton of New House, Sutton, who sub-let it to Thomas Coolbear. William Hugh Rankin (1800-72) had a daughter, Rebecca, born in 1831, who married Cockerton. Rankin purchased the farm in 1858[20] when it was put up for sale (under the terms of his son-in-law's will) at Garraway's Coffee House, Change Alley, Cornhill, London. A house with bailiff's cottage, outbuildings and stables, a well and a pump, was on the inventory, with the extent of the land given as 63 acres 3 roods 24 poles.

Another of his daughters, Elizabeth, was the first wife of Thomas King, surgeon of Rochford. At the *Old Ship* on Thursday, 21 July 1898,[21] R. Horner bought it for £900.

Apparently the farm was called Goldlord very early, becoming Goldlordcross and then Goldyng Cross. It was given in 1248 as the home of Gilbert de Goldlord. It was suggested he took his name from a treasure hoard discovered nearby, but this has not been substantiated.

Gusted Hall

Crested, Guested, and Christal Hall were other names for this farm situated behind 'The Lawn', off Hall Road. In 1338 it was cultivated by Peter Gristede from whom it was supposed to have taken its name. Thomas Darcie, who died 23 December 1485, held it, followed by his son, and then, Roger, of the family from the Earl of Ormond, lord of the manor. Roger died 3 September 1508.[22] William Harrys was here in 1556[23] when he held it from Lord Rich; Christopher, of the same family, who died in 1570, came next, leaving it to his son of the same Christian name, who died in the following year. A child of three, William was the inheritor, but before he died in 1634, he had been knighted. Afterwards his cousin, Christopher, succeeded to the title.

A gap followed, for the next owner found was John Saward (1739-81). Mrs. Mary Blackthorne, whose death occurred on 20 July 1827, held it, but it was not until 1840 that more information was found, for in that year it was occupied by John Alliston, when it contained 135 acres, said Benton. One of its most interesting owners followed, for on 5 July 1856, George Wood, a Rochford solicitor, took Gusted Hall over from Stephen James Woodthorpe. Wood had already bought other smaller farms around, so he became quite a landowner. He was a great gardening enthusiast and had the Hall laid out with semi-tropical plants and shrubs. At the house he built up an extensive library of books on horticulture and other topics. When he died on 15 November 1877 they fetched a fine price of £770, when sold in Chelmsford, for there were by then over 3,000 volumes. His trustees sold the farm to Abraham Bernard Luck from Lewisham on Monday, 8 August 1881,[24] at Tokenhurst Yard, London. The total area was given as 221 acres 1 rood 24 poles, but this included another farm called New England. The Hall had on the ground floor two parlours, pantry, washhouse and copper, while the upper floor contained four bedrooms, with other agricultural buildings outside, the whole being part of the copyhold of the manor of Rochford Hall. One further sale I have traced, for, together with New England, it was sold in 1900 for £2,600.

Pelhams

Also on Hall Road and roughly opposite to Evan's farm was Pelhams. This, too, had other names, being called Beavoir or Bowers. Anne Wynne held it in 1840[25] after her husband John had died. Thomas Worrin of the Temple, Sutton, bought it and passed it on to Sarah, his eldest daughter. A much later owner was J. Price from 1914 to 1918.

New England

This was north of Gusted Hall. Ark Lane carried on round the back of 'The Lawn' then a branch cut off just before Gusted in a north-easterly direction to this farm. It was sold in 1833[25] to William Stevens for £1,820, when it contained a dwelling house with a labourer's cottage, a farm with outbuildings, in all some 116 acres, but a year later John

Ricketts and Stephen Collier were also there. Previously it was in the possession of Stephen Leven of Great Wakering, who died just before 1827, when he had let the farm to Thomas Fulford. Afterwards John Copland was next there. On Friday, 16 January 1846[27] at the *Bell* inn, Chelmsford, New England was purchased by George Wood for £730, a farmhouse, outbuildings and land which comprised 32 acres in all. James Moss then had it on lease of Rochford Hall. On 17 July 1857 Thomas Ricketts of Shopland had it together with Flemings, a nearby farm. On 10 October 1877 the two were sold to Norman and William Russell for £4,750.

Flemings

This farm was so often sold with its partner above, that it was difficult to separate the two, as in the 1833 sale, for Steven's also bought this from the Fulford estate. The pair cost £1,820[28] for a combined total of 111 acres. A part of this single farm was called Truss's, presumably after a previous tenant, Charles Truss, who on 8 February 1776 surrendered a piece called Lyons Underwoods to the steward of the manor of Eastwoodbury. Mark Lay had Truss's farm later, and when he died on 8 January 1802 he left it to his daughter, Sarah. The messuage there was later in the occupation of the widow Saward.

Blatches

In Cherry Orchard Lane, and about a mile due west of the house of that name, the farm of Blatches stood. It was again part of the 1833 sale and was likewise purchased by William Stevens. It contained 101 acres, and cost £2,700.[29] Tom Ricketts was a previous owner and a relative of his, John sold it on 7 November 1867[30] to John Offord.

Tapes

Lot 22 in the great sale of the Tylney Long estate was this farm, also called Stapes. It had been let to Meeson, and was bought by George Wood for £260.[31]

Pipehorns

This was lot 4 of the Fulford estate sold in 1833, and bought by Stevens for £700, where it comprised 24 acres 3 roods 15 poles. Charles Truss and Joseph Round had been previous tenants, whilst in 1789 it was with Thomas Sopwith, then John Lucking, until Thomas Fulford took it on 4 October 1815.

Chapter Twenty

OLD BUILDINGS IN ROCHFORD

The Old Moot House

IN SOUTH STREET, on the east side was a very old house, often given this name. It was built in the 15th century[1] with a central hall open to the roof and a north–south cross-wing. In the later 16th century a first floor was inserted, whilst today a modern addition has been made to back and front. It stands opposite the old county court, and was believed to be the oldest surviving house in Rochford. Despite much rebuilding it still retained, up to 1969, the curved supporting braces to the interior, with most of the original chimney stack. It had two bays with a central king-pin truss and two bow windows which jutted out over the path. It stood empty for several years, then its new owner took the windows back to conform with the line of the front wall. Large plain panes were then added in place of the lattice ones. It was thought to have been used as the moot hall before the county court was built, but what is not generally known is that an ancient reredos was found here when the Rev. J. W. Hayes and Rev. E. Smith of the Essex Archarological Society examined the place. They said the house had 11 rooms and that the reredos was like one found in a house called 'Reynolds' of nearby Prittlewell. The Hedgecocks were here before 1859 (see chapter on More Traders of the Town); afterwards the Rev. W. Nixon came in 1894.

The China Store

This was a long, narrow building, opposite Warren's showrooms, West Street, which became an estate office in 1967 and was altered when Bradley Way was made. Its side faced the road, but its long front carried on down to the brook. Mr. Willans, the grocer next door, had it built as a china shop and it was supervised by Miss Pitt. It became an estate agency for a few years and then a florist's shop.

'Freeman's Cottages'

Noble, in 1867,[2] wrote of six cottages which he placed at the end of the High Street, as South Street was often called. He said 'these had a small stone with the date 1786 and initials W.E. on, near the centre'. In September 1968 I managed to find this stone, still there, but covered over with dirt, just to the right of the door now numbered four: it had a Phoenix insurance sign by the side of it. From an old document dated 1837,[3] I found there were once 10 cottages here, so this sign was in the middle of them. The property at that time was in the possession of J. and W. Freeman, wheelwrights.

'Acacia House'

This was built in 1882 as a residence for Thomas Quy, the ironmonger next door, and it has that date on its side, but there is a piece of an older house round the back, with dates of 1837 cut into several bricks. Lieut.-Colonel Arthur Sutherland Macartney had it later, and he was the one who had the Corn exchange altered internally so that it could be used as a clubroom and gymnasium. In 1895[4] it was bought by Charlotte Horlock to house a hundred inmates from the Greenwich Union. On 11 October 1904[5] the workhouse children were moved to it as a temporary measure, then on 11 October 1907 it was purchased from Miss Potter's trustees for £750 by the Union.

'Ash Cottage'

Near the end of North Street on the west side is a high wooden house, built by William Bishop, the draper, in 1881. He was given special permission by the council of 2 November[6] of that year to break under the footpath to provide himself with a coalhouse, which he did to the extent of six feet.

'Vine Cottage'

At the end of West Street stood this small house which adjoined Lavender Square. It was occupied by Simmonds, the veterinary surgeon, for many years, then Mrs. Dennish, his sister came to live there. It had a V-shaped channel running under the floorboards, and Jack Topsfield, who told me of this said that it was free of weeds when he went to check on the fall to the brook. He presumed it was an off-shoot of the stream which came down the Drive, before that was built, and on across the Union meadow, under his father's shop (the blacksmith) and under the road to the brook. It took its name from a well-established vine that grew over the front door.

'The Lavenders'

I recalled this house in the chapter on education when it was much, much larger, with 11 rooms to the house, as well as others in outbuildings around. Like many others in Rochford it was built straight on to the soil, with no foundations, whilst its walls were largely made of lath and plaster, over wire netting. Dr. Grabham had it before 1823 and after 1832;[7] Captain Robert Augustus Bradshaw of Chelmsford was in possession on 4 October 1835. About the same time the stables were rented by Hugh Brady, a horse dealer, whilst another portion of the house was used by William Gregson, the local solicitor. An old document[8] gave Dr. Grabham's dates as 30 June 1832, and continued by saying it was first in Barnes, then Griffiths, then in Fragniere. After Grabham died, his wife and daughter stayed on at the house. Then came Gregson, the solicitor, followed by the Goddards from 1907 to 1921. Their daughter, Mrs. Stout, of 1 Ashingdon Road, gave me this information. From 1930 to 1937 it was used by nurses from the hospital, but for the last 12 years it has become a surgery.

'The Hollies'

The old house fronting on the north side of West Street and roughly in the middle of the narrow portion bore this name. It was mainly Georgian with a classical porch and was divided into three parts as spoken in other chapters on the post office and Traders (tailors). From 1905 to 1956 Arthur Cook lived here, he being the son of F. T. Cook, the South Street baker. Arthur became articled to George Wood, the solicitor, ending up as his chief clerk, and also became chairman of the Rochford council.

'Enigma House'

This building once stood in North Street, where the present entrance to the hospital is. John Potter, the grocer, from further down the street, occupied it for many years. It, too, stood on the soil without foundations. Sergeant Rennet moved in when the police station became the post office in 1926.

The Court House

On the east side of South Street stands this building erected in 1859 at the cost of £3,000. It was used by the Rochford council as their main office until they moved over to newer premises higher up the street. T. Offin used part of this old building before moving a couple of doors up to the present office.

'Osborne House'

This old house, now numbered 32 North Street, stands quite close to the old bakery. The bosses on the end of tie-bars can be clearly seen on the outside brickwork shaped like capital 'Ss', which is rather a coincidence, for a man called Independent Smith owned it for many years. He was a tall man, who invariably wore a velvet smoking cap about the house.[9]

'The Lawn'

This house has been mentioned several times under this title, but it was once called 'Stroud Green House', standing in that part of the town. It was set well back off the Hall Road, just before the turn to the Hall and Rochford. Originally a farmhouse, part housed Mother Shipton's inn. The coach road from Rayleigh used to skirt the common that lay in front of the house. Backhouse Carr was a magistrate here as early as 1772 and in 1778.[10] The estate then contained 90 acres, but more was added by the family successors. George Davis Carr was here in 1803,[11] followed by A. Tawke in 1816; it was then that the road was altered.

On 26 July 1895[12] 'The Lawn' was offered for sale with lot 1, describing the house as having dining room, sitting room, drawing room, library and kitchen, with 10 bedrooms and two dressing rooms upstairs, plus a coach house and farm premises, some 40 acres of pasture and 43 acres of rough shooting. The selling price was £3,600. In the next year[13] extra rooms were added to the house, which nowadays belongs to Maitland Keddie, who owned the large departmental store in Southend. It is a handsome whitewashed building of two storeys with five bays, in late Georgian style with an Ionic porch.

The Corn Exchange

While not exactly a house, this was built in 1866, with Francis Chancellor as architect, on the south side of West Street, just by the bank. A limited company was formed with W. T. Meeson and Rankin, the miller, as its chief supporters. Samples of wheat from the fine agricultural land around were taken there for verification, Thursday being the general day since it had the market and the farmers at the same time. It ceased in this trade in 1914, then was taken over by Miss Tawke. In 1918 Bob Gray had it for a garage and repair workshop, but gave up a couple of years later when it was carried on by Francis and Baker. The Womens' Institute began in 1922 and had various premises before renting the Exchange for a time, until they finally purchased it in 1931. The upper part of the north gable was continued to take a circular arch over the clock. To mark the occasion of the Jubilee of Queen Victoria, this clock was made double faced and hung on a strong bracket over the street.

Custom House

On the north side of Weir Pond Road and close to the old Maltings was Custom House. Its name and purpose posed a question, since Rochford is at least a mile away from navigable water. H.M. Customs and Excise branch gave me some information in October 1967,[14] 'the town was, in the 19th century, a creek of the port of Maldon and only coastwise ships went there. One customs officer was housed there and he used a room at his residence for which he was paid the sum of £4 per year'. On 6 March 1832,[15] George Ventriss was appointed 'Principal Coast Officer (Customs) at Rochford, in the port of Maldon'. James Richmond followed from 1845 to 1867, and was succeeded by Charles Eves to 1878. I found no other name until Kelly in 1882[16] recorded the name of T. H. Burbrook, but no entry was found in the next directory of 1886. The house was mainly of wood construction, old timbers being re-used, and was probably built in the late 17th century.

'Malting Cottages'

Again on Weir Pond Road these were built to house workmen for the maltings behind. The cottages and kiln were owned in the 18th century by Golden Nehemiah.[17] In 1893 they were held by Golden W. Prentice, a retired man who lived in Rayleigh. He had a famous son, Samuel, who became a lawyer and Queen's Counsel, and later was made Recorder for Maidstone. He was likewise a judge at Bow and Shoreditch county courts, and chairman of Middlesex sessions. William Bellingham and George Brunton, the latter from Rayne, were the next owners, followed by W. T. Meeson. D. H. Burles in 1939[18] said 'these houses on the north side of the road were probably built in the 17th century in two periods and were constructed in wood, rendered externally with plaster, with a deep roof of red tiles and red chimney stacks, the central one having a moulded canopy at the base'. They were pulled down in January 1952. Meeson housed workmen from his farm here, whilst he used the kiln behind them to store carts, wheat and other cereals and root crops. The kiln had a cowled top to swing in the wind. Even today the bottom floor of the old kiln remains.

Chapter Twenty-One

POSTAL SERVICES

THE DEVELOPMENT of the postal services in Essex was revealed in a series of records called the Postmaster General's reports, and from other items such as postal maps, which showed the circulation of letters to and from London. The despatch of letters was a very old custom, but the practice of dating the covers of letters would appear to have been in existence since the days of Henry VIII, according to John Hendy.[1] He wrote about the case where Thomas Cromwell complained of the slow delivery of messages to which Sir Brian Tuke, Master of the Posts, replied in 1533.

In my first chapter I wrote about the importance of the Rochford Hundred to London. As people began to move about more freely and fresh industries grew up in other parts of Essex, this, together with the emergence of importance in the seaside town of Southend, made the growth of the post in the county as rapid as any in other parts of England. Rochford shared in this development, for where commerce, trade and industry were found so people gathered, and a service was needed. Dendy Marshall[2] made Rochford a receiving town as early as 1786 and a postal town by 1820. Again in 1791[3] the London mail was sent to and from Brentwood, the controlling town, three times a week: on Sundays, Wednesdays and Fridays at 10 a.m., and arrived back there at 2 p.m. Letters were then brought to Rochford for onward delivery to other places around, such as Prittlewell, Leigh, Southchurch, Wakering and Barling.

George Poulton[4] was Rochford's earliest-named postmaster, who did his normal work of receiving and sorting at an inn (the name was not given) after he had collected it from Brentwood. He also undertook the riding work involved from this very important bye-post. For this duty he received a salary of £37 per annum, but added to it by receiving a half share in the penny delivery fee raised on all letters and newspapers he handled, also from those he collected en route, for which he was allowed a full penny charge. His ride from Brentwood took in the towns of Billericay, Wickford, Rayleigh, and Hockley, a distance of 18 miles to Rochford. In 1795,[5] riding hard from South End with a government express letter, he broke his leg at Ramsden Crays, for which he was granted five guineas for medical aid and for his fare home, but this was 'only on compassionate grounds' the post office authorities said. By 1802 the frequency of the post had become doubled to six times per week, and in 1805[6] the revenue from Rochford was put at £700 per year; so in that year the surveyor of posts recommended its upgrading to independent general post town. However, the postmaster, a Mr. Cooledge, was not considered fit to undertake the higher responsibilities of a post town. He was said to be illiterate and apt to leave many duties to his wife, nor was an inn considered a proper place for the post. So Thomas White, a leather cutter, was appointed in his place. William Kernott, the market place druggist, John Barrington, of Great Doggett's farm, and Thomas Swain, surgeon, were his sureties.

At this time the fifth clause post arrangements were introduced, which meant the connection of small villages and towns with the General Post network, providing the

Postal Services 145

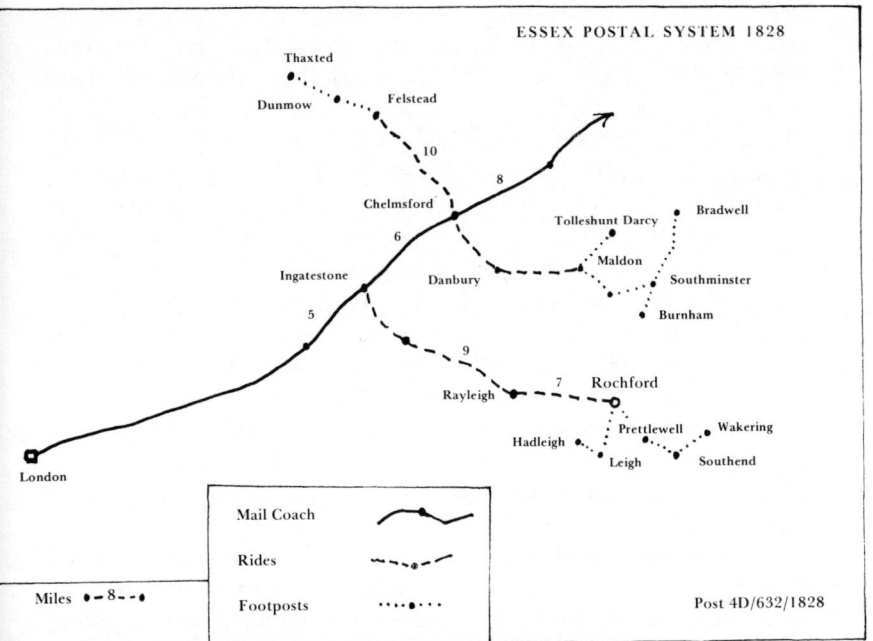

Fig. 10a

Fig. 10b Postmarks for 1823/4 and 1841

traffic sent was at least enough to make the post self-supporting. In the Rochford area, under this new arrangement the post office itself was to benefit from the pence obtained from local letters, which hitherto had been enjoyed by Cooledge and other local postmasters. Henceforth the postal charge for every letter was to be fourpence. Again the timetable of the Brentwood to Wakering post was rearranged so that the mail cart left Brentwood during the night and arrived at Rochford at four o'clock in the morning. By this earlier despatch the mail cart driver lost his former advantages of carrying parcels along the way. For this he was compensated by being made guard of the mail with a wage of 14s. a week. From Rochford, a foot messenger, walking 20 miles a day, carried the mail to Southend and Wakering, for which arduous duty he received 19s. a week.

All was not well, however, for on 3 February 1813,[7] George Western wrote from Wakering and proposed that the post from Rochford and around be reconverted to a penny post. The letter was addressed to Mr. Freeling at the General Post Office. He, in turn wrote to the House of Lords[8] the next day and commented on the suggestion. He said the post had been difficult to manage: 'there being often objections made to the extra penny on putting letters into the receiving boxes, a restriction that is a check to correspondence and of course injurious to the revenue'. He went on to say he enclosed Mr. Western's letter 'whose proposal to use the more simple Penny post by which the boxes will be open and the high rate of 4d. on what was termed short letters be reduced', he supported. He continued by saying that the franks and newspapers would be chargeable and by this he thought the revenue would gain. He carried on by saying that he had given these new instructions to the surveyors for the postmasters and receivers, to save time. He trusted that as no additional expenses were involved the Lords would agree.

In 1816 the Wakering post began from Ingatestone instead of Brentwood and so things continued smoothly until 1822. In that year, Joshua Westhorpe, a new driver of the Rochford mail cart, was stopped one night by three highwaymen as he was turning off the Billericay road, en route to Ingatestone. His courage and the sound of approaching horses scared them off, and although he was stunned by a blow from a stick, he recovered his balance and drove hell for leather to his destination. A reward of £50 was offered for the capture of the miscreants, but this was never claimed.[9]

Two years later,[10] Rochfordians were again complaining about the penny delivery fee charged by the postmaster on letters delivered to their homes. Mr. White defended himself by saying that when he was appointed, this charge was regularly levied on letters delivered, and that the surveyor had promised he could continue to take it, unless the people of Rochford refused to pay up. If they did, he was told, the Postmaster General might consider granting him an allowance to employ a letter carrier. This was done, and a sum of 5s. a week was granted, for him to employ such a person to give a free delivery within the confines of the town. Rayleigh, which had also begun to grow in size and importance complained on the same lines in 1827, and got free delivery, but their carrier only obtained 2s. 6d. per week.

By the mid-1840s[11] the Eastern Counties railway had replaced the London to Norwich mail coach which stopped off at Brentwood and Ingatestone to leave the Rochford and district mail. A mail cart, however, now carried its mail over the road from Chelmsford and Ingatestone, and then on to Rochford, but the foot messenger was still in use from here.

In 1880 a change was made and the mail began to come from the *Queen's Head* inn, Chelmsford.

As said, the inn was the earliest record of an office in Rochford, but later it is believed Thomas White used his own house. After that an old thatched house, situated behind 'Ash Cottage' in North Street was used. This had a floor of beaten earth which dropped down some eight inches from the outside level[12] to the living or post room. When Henry Wood took over as postmaster in 1852 he used the part of 'The Hollies', in West Street, now numbered 46, as the office, and had a hole cut in the wall to conduct the business.[13] In 1867 Jesse D. Garrood was in charge and he transferred the office to his ironmongery shop across the same street.

In turn, F. W. Francis, the printer, took over in 1892, using the same house for the postal trade, and the next for his own works. He had the house after that, now No. 45, then called 'Franklyn House', as his private residence. The posting box was outside in the wall of the post office. I walked down the street in June 1971 and found the box still there, although boarded over. Finally the office was moved to North Street.

The obliterating number 651 was allotted to Rochford in 1786, said Dendy Marshall. The example shown with the word Rochford and number 44 beneath was a mileage mark, which were phased out *c.* 1829. The other illustration was in use from that date.

Chapter Twenty-Two

MISS TAWKE

MISS AUGUSTA S. TAWKE, who was born in 1856 and died in 1947, was much given to hunting and social activities. In 1913 she wrote her *Hunting Recollections,* although they were not published until 1924, and then in four slim volumes. She had already established a home for wayward girls in Hockley in 1909 with the help of some generous friends. The money from the sale of her book furthered the cause. The home was used as a means of shelter and as a place of refuge for girls in difficult circumstances and for those unable to find work. After a trial period at the house, positions were found for those deemed worthy, mainly as maids and servants in Rayleigh, Hockley and Rochford. Miss Tawke herself lived then at Bulwood Hall, close to Rayleigh, where the house had space for such a project. It is a great coincidence that today her old residence is used by H.M. government as a remand home for young women.

Although most of her books were about fox hunting, she wrote of many personalities from the surrounding district. In Volume 1 she spoke of Tom Offin, a well-known local name, for there is a firm of Offin and Rumsey today in Rochford. He was the master of the South-east Essex foxhounds, and John Offin held the same office from 1869-73. In the next volume she said, 'Miss Boosey was at the hunt on wheels' and 'Master Tabor was there also'.

These names are connected with old Rochford families. This meet was started off at Sutton Ford bridge on October 1880, and the hounds stayed at the *Old Ship* inn on the 19th of that month.

She wrote about 'Old Mrs. Swaine [the doctor's wife] who used to drive to dinner along Ironwell Lane [then the main road through to Hockley] and on to London . . . where the coach often used to get stuck in the mud so that the journey had to be completed on foot'. The Scratton family remembered in connection with Prittlewell Priory found a place in her book, and she had a word or two to say about the coming of the railway to Rochford. She lamented that the coating of Kentish rag (stone) was a luxury on the roads.

Mr. and Mrs. Wilson were the first workhouse master and matron she knew. They were, in fact, the fourth in that office, for they came on 28 August 1850. Their son later became the founder of the firm of land and estate agents now called Watson, Temple and Weymouth of Southend. The Taylors, the Grosvenors and Mr. and Mrs. Moss were later in charge of the Union. In that she was correct. She managed to get the children from that building admitted to the board school, before which they had been proverbial prisoners, shut up in the high walls of the Union. Their only relaxation had been the walk outside twice a week, when they were marched two by two for a bare half-hour. This was one of the few times when brother and sister might meet, apart from which they were segregated from the moment they entered the establishment. It was Miss Meeson of Doggett's farm who obtained red flannel for the females to have nightgowns, wrote Miss Tawke. The poor girls wore cotton garments both winter and summer, and boys and girls were often dressed alike up to five years old, to save

Miss Tawke 151

expense. More than that, no pocket handkerchief was allowed to anyone, to save both money and laundry. She said that the master's house was a square building in the centre of the grounds with a hipped roof to the corners, save at the top where a clock tower stopped the ends from meeting. The clock had four faces and struck the hours with a bell.

She reminisced about a certain young man who stayed at her new home, 'The Lawn', off Hall Road, where she came after her grandfather had bought the place from G. D. Carr. He was very particular about his clothes, she remarked, and had a different suit for every occasion, including one for attending Rochford market. On the 18 December 1897 a meet was held at Rochford Hall with Poyser's harriers, and in the following year, she went on to say, on 8 June, Hawkwell Hall was the rendezvous, when the hare broke early and went to the back of Swaine's farm, then carried on to Doggett's (farm), through to Stambridge Hall and Little Doggetts before it continued on to Ashingdon church.

Mr. Montague was curate at Hawkswell church when Mr. Kemp was the vicar, and she called Mr. Bristow, who owned land at Stroud Green, 'the Bishop of Essex'. He was, 'in the forage business', she wrote. Between 1910 and 1914, she had the Corn Exchange converted into a laundry, after it had been a garage and repair workshop, where some of her 'strays' were provided both with an occupation and some wages.

Chapter Twenty-Three

THE INNS OF ROCHFORD

THERE IS NO DOUBT that some of these houses were very old. Although few details exist prior to *c.* 1590 a record taken two years later for the Hundred of Rochford said there were four alehouses in the town, and one inn. No place was named, but one landlord was identified as Robert Brook. John Taylor published a book in 1637 called *Cosmographia,* wherein he listed Judith Rix as an innkeeper at Rochford.

The *Old Ship*
There are two houses in Rochford with the word 'Ship' in their title. This one, in North Street, has its side on the lane bearing the same name. Ind Coope of Romford, are the present owners, though it has had many in its very long existence. They have a record of 6 January 1670 declaring Edward Paine in charge. It goes on to say that Richard Finch was before him, also Thomas Horne, and before that Thomas Sloan, whilst John England, the elder, sold it to Dorothy Atkinson on the '6 and 20th day of January in the two and fortieth year of the Lady Elizabeth, Queen of England'. This would make the date 1600 exactly. It has another claim to fame, if such a word can be used; for connected with it were the last two men to be hanged for sheep stealing in England, on 24 March 1820.[1]

On that date Thomas Fairhead and Henry Gilliott died on the scaffold in the yard of Moulsham Gaol, Chelmsford.

The Inns of Rochford

The former had a butcher's stall in the yard of the *Old Ship*, the latter being a shepherd for Thomas Large at Prittlewell Priory, where the offence occurred. Fairhead was engaged to Mary Waters, daughter of the landlord, who, poor girl, died of a broken heart. Both men were under 24, said Benton, who also mentioned that, at the end, Gilliott took the blame. It was owned before 1838[2] by Francis Hardcastle, M.P., but later it belonged to Francis Lamberth with John Waters proprietor in 1793,[3] his wife, Mary, in 1828,[4] and Robert Bright in 1832.[5] In 1838[6] Bright was still here, but after this the landlord was Thomas Marks in 1845.[7]

The *New Ship*

This inn, only a few yards away, and almost at the other end of Old Ship Lane, is covered by deeds from 1733 to 1818[8] at the Essex Record Office. In 1793 Samuel Wade was here, with George Arnold in 1823, but probably one of its most noted landlords was Henry Prior, spoken of in another chapter, who had charge from 1868 to 1886, followed by his wife for several years. There is a car park today on the side, where several houses once stood, with two on the East Street and three or four rounding into the lane. It was here one of the old cannons was placed, spoken of in the chapter on King's Hill and the Whispering Court. The inn was bought in 1866[9] by Frederick and Arthur Veley of Chelmsford from Richard Hutley Crabb, brewer of Great Baddow.

The *Marlborough Head*

A deed of 19 December 1706[10] reposes in the Essex Record Office, but the inn was here long before that. Benton spoke of William Belcham, the landlord, and the hard drinkers who frequented here. First listed in 1828,[11] he died soon after in 1833. Earlier William Newman was in charge before 1793,[12] but it was spoken of by the *Chelmsford Chronicle* of 1 August 1764 as an old inn. It was probably named after the Duke, like many more at the time of his exploits. Rumour had it that Wellington quartered troops here, for the inn and neighbouring buildings were still partly connected by cellars up to late years, which might have extended to form barracks below ground. There was a lane by its side which had five houses on one side, and as many or more on the other. It had the name Barrack Lane. Major Tawke of 'The Lawn', used to drill the Yeomanry behind the inn.

The *Vernon's Head*

On the site of the Corn Exchange, West Street, now the Women's Institute, stood the *Vernon's Head*. Built c. 1741, to commemorate the exploits of Admiral Vernon (1684-1757), who captured Porto Bello in 1739. Martin Thayer was landlord in 1793[13] and Samuel Wakers in 1823/4.[14] It disappeared around 1865 as did many others similarly named when Vernon was caught up in the annihilation at Culloden, Miller Christy's *History of Industries in Essex*, published in 1907, said it had been gone for some years.

The *King's Head*

This was a well-known coaching inn, as the chapter on transport indicated. At one time it was part of the homage of the Manor Court, like the market and the Square. It was held by John Offord in 1849[15] on those terms. Ind Coope told me that they had deeds going back to 7 October 1739, and they reminded me it had originally been called the *Blue Boar* when previously owned. This must have been before 1793, since it was called *King's Head* here. The

The Inns of Rochford

supper for the latter stages of the Lawless Court took place here. Wells and Perry held it on 30 March 1850.[16]

The *Horse and Groom*

Before Rochford was enlarged this inn stood on the other side of Salt bridge and so was in Eastwood, but it had strong connections with the town because of the Hall (see chapter on the dove-cote). Its former owners have not been found, but it belonged to the Stambridge brewery, which itself has now been pulled down. J. A. Hardcastle, M.P., owned it in the years between 1842 and 1868,[17] followed by Lukers of Southend. Once the inn stood on the edge of the brook. A small house later stood here, perhaps part of the older building which was moved some 10 yards nearer to Southend. This small residence was occupied in the last years of the 19th century, and on into the next century, by Captain Strachan, a German, born in 1861, who strutted the streets of Rochford in breeches and gaiters, especially for a week or so after the arrival of his pension of £8 per month. Strangely enough I found he had English Christian names when I finally traced his burial as being at Hockley, on 3 February 1913, where Rev. Nixon, a retired clergyman, helped at the service.

The *Rose and Crown*

At the end of North Street, close to the join with Weir Pond Road, stands this inn, first called the *Crown*. Mann, Crossman and Paulin, its present owners, were unable to tell me when it was changed, but it had the addition prefixed for the first time in the 1878 directory. It had a large shed at the back in which tramps, vagrants, and sometimes performers slept. Hence it acquired a nickname, the

Pad and Can. The charge for a bed of straw was 4d. per night, but sometimes an order from the police, in the old station down the street, would suffice.

The *White Horse*
Further down North Street, past the *Rose and Crown* stood this inn which took its name like scores of others from animals. There are deeds for it from the years 1800-83 at the Essex Record Office. It belonged to Seabrooke's breweries, when it had an extra building on its end, making it like a letter L. Harry Chapman told me his mother stayed there when told to leave by Monday morning after her husband had died on the Thursday. Chapman, senior, had lived in the steward's cottage at the Hall.

The *Cock* Inn
On the Hall Road, just before the bend, stands the *Cock* inn. In the days before 1850 it was listed as in Stroud Green. Mann, Crossman and Paulin, its present owners, have a reference to it for 1777. They told me H. Woodston was here in 1810, with Charles Price from 1856 to 1888, and H. Thorrington in 1908. It probably replaced *Mother Shipton's* inn. (See 'The Lawn'.)

The *Three Ashes*
This was here, on the beginning of Sutton Road, before the *Anne Boleyn*. Like the *Horse and Groom* it was then in Eastwood parish. Two bungalows on the south side, built in 1967, stand on the spot. John Gladwell was here in 1823/4[18] and recorded up to 1890[19] but it might have been a son here in the latter years. He had a niece, E. James, and a housekeeper, Miss Livermore, who assisted him. He

The Inns of Rochford

farmed the land round the inn and brewed his own ale in a barn behind the house. It was the property of Lydia May Mayer, who marrie John Heathcote of Connington Hall, Huntngdonshire, on 6 June 1811. After Gladwell left, it became a farmhouse and was kept as such by Walter Bridge until 1901, when it was sold on 25 September.[20]

The *Anne Boleyn*

When the *Three Ashes* was sold the licence was transferred here.[21] It was then called a hotel, but had been spelt in many ways, particularly in old English. A notable record was that of the How family who ended 46 years of proprietorship on 15 October 1969.

The *Golden Lion*

This, now a free house, stands a few yards further down North Street, on the same side as the *Prince of Wales*. W, Barnes had it in 1874, with Fred Crowe, the plumber next for the years 1886-1909, and A. Warner, another plumber, following him. Was this place the *Red Lion,* a former inn whose deeds of 1713 were placed in the Record Office? Messrs. Wells and Perry, who were the forerunners of Taylor and Walker, held it for some years until it was sold in October 1961 to a private tenant.

The *Prince of Wales*

There were several places selling beer besides inns. This shop, in North Street, was part-butcher and part alehouse. John Lindsell had it in 1900, followed in 1908 by J. and C. Searle, in whose possession it continued up to 1940, when A. Ferguson arrived to take it over as a butchery only.

The *Star* inn

In the Market Square corner, where for many years a stationery and newspaper shop had stood was this inn, which ceased after the 1884 fire.

Lukers

Another off-licence house stood halfway down West Street on the north side. This was used mainly as a store, a kind of half-way place for distribution of barrels and kegs from the main brewery in Alexandra Street, Southend. The house is believed to be the one numbered fifty-two.

The *Eel Hole*

A place with this interesting name,[22] stood some distance down Watts Lane. It was a wooden building pulled down c. 1889, although it had ceased in its beer trade some years earlier and had been made into two cottages. It got its name from a large hole nearby connected to the brook from which eels could be taken.

Chapter Twenty-Four

THE HOSPITALS

JUST AS THERE WERE three bridges associated with the town, so there were three hospitals connected with it. The first of these was called the Outer hospital, and took in patients with smallpox, a disease that had always been rife in early times. This place stood some distance behind Guested Hall, but was best reached by going by way of Fleming's farm. Its exact location was recorded as in Noble's Green, just north of Green Lane, which is today off the present Eastwood Road, Southend. Later it was called the Infectious Diseases hospital, but the names were so interchanged with the other sick institutions that information was often confused. A note in an early minute book of the council, dated 4 August 1857, stated that Thomas Rider had put in a tender for £2,777 for a hospital which was accepted, but nothing apparently was done about it, for this hospital was not built until 1904.[1] It was a small building, somewhat like a country chapel, and had four tiny wards, with an outbuilding for emergencies. Hedges were planted on three sides, with the fourth strung with wire. It remained empty for many years and was finally pulled down in 1939/40 after being permanently closed in 1935. The materials were brought back to Rochford depot and used to construct a garage. A well was dug on 16 August 1904 by S. Norden, the builder, at a cost of £13.

The second hospital was called the Fever hospital, and was a semi-wooden building erected in the grounds of Swaine's farm by permission of W. T. Meeson. A council minute, dated 3 December 1873[2] gave him permission to enclose part of the land for this purpose, but nothing was done for a time since a later minute of 12 November 1889[3] said the hospital was established in 1878. It was short-lived since Meeson was given six months' notice on 18 March 1890[4] that the hospital building would be vacated on Lady Day 1891. However, on 17 March 1891[5] Meeson was asked to allow the institution to continue for a further six months to Michaelmas, but another report on 22 January 1902[6] said two cases of smallpox had been sent there, and a couple of months later, on 4 March 1902[7] a marquee, costing £122, was erected on the grounds because of another smallpox outbreak. Mr. and Mrs. Emma Lacey were caretaker and matron on 3 February 1891[8] after Mrs. Shelley had resigned.

It was about this time, after many arguments, that the Sutton Ford hospital was founded. All in all, it had taken 35 years to come to fruition, as it had been mooted at the time of the temporary building at Swaine's. In 1891[9] Stallebrass of Eastwoodbury had written a letter, dated 16 June, to the council, offering to sell two acres of land on the west side of a 12-acre field at Purdy's farm, Sutton. The price agreed was £250, and on 12 February 1895[10] the land was conveyed to the Rochford council for that sum. However, delay occurred, and it was not until 22 January 1901 that S. Norden's tender for £3,810 for building the hospital was accepted. It, too, was called the Infectious Diseases hospital. By the time it was finished, alterations and additions had pushed the cost up by another thousand pounds. Charles M. Thompson was named as witness in a case brought by Charlotte Horlock of 'Acacia

House' against the Rev. B. Cotton, who had previously asked for extra fees for burying her inmates, then later refused to inter any more, and finally was said to have struck one of them on 13 August 1895.[11] Thompson and his wife were the first caretaker and nurse for the hospital. At one time the place could be reached by way of Tinker's Lane, some 30 yards beyond the *Horse and Groom,* but later the lane was barred off and access was only obtained from Sutton Road. The hospital stood off a small side road just before the bridge.

Chapter Twenty-Five

POPULATION

IN 1801, THE FIRST CENSUS was taken, but this was only a general count of numbers. It was not until 1841 that any actual attempt was made to obtain other facts, such as trades. To obtain an earlier figure for the population of Rochford, I turned to the Hearth Tax for 1671.[1]

No. of Hearths	Houses	Hearths	Houses	Hearths	Houses
11	1	7	2	3	13
10	0	6	0	2	25
9	1	5	3	1	38
8	1	4	18	Total	102

Further information was given that nine persons were in receipt of alms and therefore not included, nor were the inhabitants of Rochford Hall, though this was quoted as having 32 hearths. I assumed each pauper had a domicile and added these 9 to the 102 above, to give a total of 111 households.

Many local historians have devised formulae for use with the Hearth Tax figures, and for other returns, notably Dr. K. H. Burley.[2] The numbers they have taken vary between three and seven persons per house. I felt the average between these numbers, viz., five, to be a useful trial figure. Using this, my 111 households gave me 555 people. To this I added

Population 163

35, an estimate of the number at the Hall, comprised of the family and servants. This gave me a grand total of five hundred and ninety.

Benton,[3] however, quoted 180 dwelling houses for the 1801 census figures of 1,228 people, which gave an average of 6.8 per household. I tried again with the 1821 return, where the given number was 1,382 people for 196 houses, which gave a mean value of just over seven per home.

I felt, therefore, that my 1671 figure of 590 was too low, using five as my multiplier, so I took a final figure of 5.5, which gave me 610, to which was added the same 35 people estimated at the Hall, making 645 in all. I felt this compared more favourably with an estimated 700[4] for approximately a hundred years later, for the cloth trade, which had been one of the staple trades of Essex, had begun to decline by the end of the 17th century, and by the middle of the next 100 years was drawing to a close. This meant that a rise of only 55 people in 100 years made my estimate a very reasonable one.

I attributed the slow rise in the population between 1801 and 1831 to other factors. The rise in popularity of both Southend and London, the former because of higher wages, new buildings which offered work, trade and money, and because of the royal patronage it was given, coupled with its increased favour as a seaside town, and the capital city for similar reasons regarding buildings, but also because many wealthy households were offering quarters as well as wages for both men and women, even if many were only as servants. With the 1801 census,[5] Rochford, fortunately, recorded its population together with a little additional information, giving 216 people engaged in agricultural pursuits, and 111 persons in trades or professions.

Another check on the population was made from the Invasion returns of 1803,[6] where Schedule No. 1 gave the following figures:—

Names of Men, 15-60 yrs.	Incapable	Serving as Volunteers or Armed Associations	Aliens and Quakers
250, named in Schedule 3, and comprised as follows: Infantry - - 64 Pioneers - - 119 Others serving with latter - 39 Ditto, with teams - - 22 Guides - - 6	100 persons whose names cannot be inserted for lack of space	G. D. Carr, in W. Essex Militia Wm. Pepper, Wm. Sayers, Robert Sopwith, Samuel Green, Joseph Drinkwater	None
			0
			Others who from infancy, infirmity may not be capable of removing themselves
Total - 250	100	6	859

Signed: J. Barrington, churchwarden, Ed. Codlin and John Wade, constables.

Totalling these, gave a figure of 1,251, but Rev. Wise's name was not included as he was the Pioneer General. This is a much closer comparison with the figures for 1801 (1,228) and 1811 (1,214).

Schedule No. 2, signed by the same people, gave a list of cattle and stock; Schedule No. 3 gave an inventory of Rochford people under various headings, such as team-driver, cattle-driver, pioneer, etc., with Rev. J. Wise named as

Population	165

Pioneer General. A further register was taken called the Additional Army of England, dated 30 July 1803, which had approximately 140 persons named, with their occupations given such as labourers, of which 48 were recorded, innkeepers, butchers, doctors, lawyers, etc. It was evident that these lists were carefully checked, since a fine[7] was levied on the parish for a deficiency of one man to the armed forces.

One other help was found as to the question of the population of the town, for one Monday, 27 May 1811, a further check was made by Rev. J. Wise which listed 184 people in the first column, names of families, and gave a grand total of 1,212, which again is very close to the other figures quoted.

Names of families	Houses		Families chiefly engaged			Numbers including children	
	Inhabited	By how many families	Agric.	Trade or Manuf.	Other Occup.	Male	Female
Rev. J. Wise Widow Bragg	1	1					
Ann Dissmore	1	1					
G. D. Carr	1	1					
Philip Gullock	1	1	170	139	21	606	606
etc.	etc.	etc.	Total			1,212	

On 26 August 1825 a return was made by the overseers for the parish of men qualified to serve on juries, which was signed by George Brooklehurst, draper, and Thomas

Merrifield, farmer, with the name T. Salmon as High Constable of the Hundred, in which 28 names were given with occupations and qualifications. Pigot specifically gave the population in 1831 as 1,256 inhabitants, and added the number had only increased *by 28* in the preceding 30 years;

Population Figures

Year	People	Source	Additional information
1801	1,228	Benton	180 dwelling houses. Union inmates included
1811	1,214	Benton	608 males, 606 females. Union inmates included
1821	1,382	Benton	196 houses, 284 resident families. Union inmates included
1831	1,526	Benton	763 males, 763 females, Union inmates included
1841	1,722	V.C.H.	
1851	1,704	Benton	
1861	1,696	V.C.H., Vol. 2	
1871	1,589	Directories	
1881	1,665	Benton	
1891	1,612	Directories	
1901	1,829	Directories	
1911	1,821	Directories	
1921	2,077	Directories	
1931	3,009	Directories	
1939	4,000	Directories	
1941	no census		
1951	6,049	Directories	
1961	7,806	Directories	
1971	Over 8,000	Rochford Council	

Population

The following table[10] gives some indication of the cholera epidemic of 1847-49.

Average Annual Death Rate of England and Wales.

1841-45	..	21.40 per 1,000	Birth rate 32,36 per 1,000
1846-50	..	23.34 per 1,000	Birth rate 32.83 per 1,000
1851-55	..	22.70 per 1,000	Birth rate 33.90 per 1,000

The emigration figures are given for similar years in the next table.

Year	People	Year	People	Year	People	Year	People
1833	62,527	1839	62,207	1845	93,501	1851	335,966
1834	76,222	1840	90,743	1846	129,851	1852	368,764
1835	44,478	1841	118,592	1847	258,270	1853	329,937
1836	75,417	1842	128,344	1848	248,089	1859	323,429
1837	72,034	1843	57,212	1849	299,498	1855	176,807
1838	33,222	1844	70,686	1850	280,849		

Possible these, too affected the numbers for Rochford, but three other factors certainly did. First, in trying to establish certain dates,I examined many gravestones, where I noted numerous early deaths, especially of females. Coupled with this was the fact that many men were married twice or more, and third, as Essex was largely an agricultural county the low wages of the farm labourers (they were quoted by Bodey as 9s. 0d. per week in 1774[11]) did not make for a large population.

There are surely other factors that had a bearing on the low or slow increase in the town's population but I will only take one more, from Benton, for he made a specific point in his figures for 1811, quoting 608 males and 606 females, a detail which needs no expansion.

Chapter Twenty-Six

CONCLUSION

I HAVE ALREADY touched on the happenings at King's Hill, for although the attempt to demolish it has temporarily failed, its present boarded-up condition can only lead to deterioration. Rochford Hall seems fairly safe with most of what remains let to the Rochford Hundred Golf Club. The old Moot house, No. 17 South Street, has been altered as I have indicated, whilst in the Square the whole of the east end has been pulled down and rebuilt in modern style, complete even to a supermarket. I can add to this list with the four cottages from East Street, Nos. 10 to 16, which were cleared away in 1958. Last, but by no means least, the old saddler's shop, dated 1777, was knocked down on Sunday, 18 March 1973, a day the developers *choose* to do their work.

So much for the ravages of time, or should it be called progress? Whatever the phrase, the increase in population, so rapid since 1940, carries on apace, and now the town is little short of 10,000 people. This alone has meant change, and the Market Square is now filled with parked cars since the cattle ceased to be sold (1959). There is so little industry in the town since the Ekco works closed, and although a small company, Matchbox Toys, took over, it employed far fewer people. The Magnolia works in Rectory Road, making mouldings and picture frames, is but a small concern.

Thus most of the people, particularly the male population, are commuters, many only to Southend, but a large number to London or towns en route to the capital. Housing for the most part has been concentrated in two areas, the Rochford Garden Way complex, and the Ashingdon Road estates. The four old streets remain, but they can no longer be truthfully called the middle of the town except for the shopping centre.

One more event might have caused a big change to Rochdord, namely the proposal by the Conservative government to site the third airport at Foulness. By inference the Southend airport, which is situated in the Rochford area would probably have closed. It was inevitable that at least one new major road would have been built from London to Foulness. This was to have run north of Rochford, but near enough to affect it in several ways. This would have meant a further and probable, rapid rise in population, with the need for more amenities, more shops and more schools, or the enlargements of existing facilities. Rochford, which so far had escaped that modern nightmare of tall buildings and high-rise flats, would probably have succumbed to the need for progress.

However, with the new political scene, the return of the Labour party in February 1974, although they were slightly in the minority, and their subsequent return in October of the same year, again with only a narrow majority, a reconsideration of the high cost has led that party to abandon the project. So, at least for some time, Rochford may escape the penalties I have outlined.

One thing is certain: the past has gone, and much that has fallen will never be replaced. Old memories, fast-fading, together with some old photographs and prints, remain for a time. If my story can but preserve some of the past history of the town then perhaps it will have been worth the endeavour.

BIBLIOGRAPHY

Main Sources

History and Antiquities of Essex (1740-42), N. Salmon.
History and Antiquities of Essex (1768), P. Morant.
A New and Complete History of Essex (1771), P. Muilman.
A New Complete History of Essex (1772), by a Gentleman.
General Review of Agriculture in Essex (1795), G. Vancouver.
Topographical and Historical Description of Essex, Brayleigh and Bratton (1803).
A Guide to the Watering and Sea Bathing Places (1806), Philips.
Topographical and Statistical Description of Essex (1807), G. A. Cooke.
Agriculture in the County of Essex (1813), A. Young.
Guide to Southend and District (1824), by a Gentleman.
History and Topography of Essex (1834), T. Wright.
People's History of Essex (1861), D. W. Coller.
Annals of Evangelical Nonconformity (1863), T. W. David.
A History of Rochford Hundred (1867), P. Benton.
The Lawless Court (1869), W. H. Black.
Origins of the Peculiar People (1882), Isaac Anderson.
Handbook of Essex (1887), Miller Christy.
History of the Peculiar People (1888), F. W. Harrad.
Bygone Essex (1892), William Andrews.
Round Southend (1893), C. R. B. Barrett.
Picturesque Essex (1905), Duncan Moul and R. Ernest Hill.
Historical Notes on Southend and District (1909), J. W. Burrows.
Miss Tawke's *Recollections* (1913).

Recollections of Jabez Francis (1916), written about 1890.
Water Supplies in Essex (1916), Dr. Thresh.
New Light on the Pilgrim Story (1920) W. T. Mason
Reminiscences of W. J. Francis (1923).
Essex: Its Forests, Folk and Folk-lore (1928), C. L. Mason.
Essex Survival (1929), F. Roe.
Peeps into the Past (1929), H. W. Tompkins.
Pigeon Cotes and Dove Cotes of Essex (1931), D. Smith.
Essex Windmills (1932), D. Smith.

Secondary Sources
Roads (1971), Hugh Bodey.
Transport and Communication (1962), N. P. Bray.
The Rolling Road (1956), L. A. G. Strong.
Economic Development of Essex, late 17th, early 18th century (1957), Dr. K. H. Burley.
English Historical Documents, Vol. XII (1), 1833-1871 (1965), D. C. Douglas, ed.
English Local Government—Poor Law History (1927), Sydney and Beatrice Webb.
The British Post Office (1926), Dendy Marshall.
History of Early Postmarks of British Isles (1905), John Hendy.
The Buildings of Essex (1965), Nikolaus Pevsner.
Royal Commission on Historical Monuments in Essex, 4 vols., 1916-23.
Sepulchral Monuments of Essex (1890), J. C. Chancellor.
Elizabethan Life—Disorder (1970), F. G. Emmison.
Repertorium Ecclesiasticum, Vol. 11 (1710), Richard Newcourt.
Essex Journal (from 1966).
Essex Almanacs (from 1872).
Transactions of Essex Archaeological Society (from 1858).
Various local newspapers.

REFERENCES

Abbreviations

S.R.L.	Southend Reference Library.
E.R.O.	Essex Record Office.
R.A.S.	Rochford Amenities Society.
P.O.	Post Office.
P.O.R.	Post Office Records.
U.B.D.	Universal British Directory (1793).
R.U.M.B.	Rochford Union Minute Book.
R.C.M.B.	Rochford Council Minute Book.

Chapter One

1. D. W. Coller, *People's History of Essex*, p. 188 (1861).
2. W. Stubbs, *Constitutional History of England* (1903).
3. D. M. Shelton, *English Society in Middle Ages*, pp. 152–3 (1951).
4. R. Arnold, *A Social History of England*, pp. 218–9 (1967).
5. A. B. Allen, *The Middle Ages, 1154–1486*, p. 248 (1957).
6. R. Arnold, *A Social History of England*, p. 223 (1967).
7. H. M. Chadwick, *Studies in Anglo-Saxon Institutions*, p. 209 (1962).
8. P. Benton, *The History of Rochford Hundred*, p. 774 (1867) (hereafter abbreviated to Benton).
9. Benton, p. 775.
10. A. D. Bayne, *Royal Illustrated History of East England*, p. 44 (n.d., c. 1900).
11. John W. Burrows, *Southend on Sea Antiquarian and Historical Transactions*, (Vol. 3 (1938), 'Local History in Pageantry, p. 152.
12. Benton, p. 776;
13. Benton, p. 777.
14. Benton, p. 795. (Some doubt exists about this date.)
15. Benton, p. 778.
16. Benton, p. 779.
17. *Ibid.*

18. Benton, p. 797.
19. Benton, p. 798.
20. E.R.O., Q/SBb44/13.
21. E.R.O., Q/SBb237/21.
22. E.R.O., Q/SBb270/49.
23. E.R.O., Q/SBb315.
24. E.R.O., Q/SBb270/26.

Chapter Two
1. T. W. Davids, *Annals of Evangelical Nonconformity*, p. 41 (1863).
2. Coller, *op. cit.*, p. 492.
3. Benton, p. 786.
4. E.R.O., T/P181/9-14.
5. E.R.O., D/DCw P13.
6. *Essex Journal*, Vol. 1, No. 1 (Jan. 1966), p. 25. Article by D. G, Macleod, M.A.
7. Miller Christy, *A Handbook of Essex* (1887).
8. E.R.O., D/DQs113/8.
9. *Ibid.*
10. Benton, p. 896.
11. T. W. Davids, *op. cit.*, p. 47.

Chapter Three
1. Benton, p. 794.
2. *Ibid.*
3. Coller, *op. cit.*, p. 493.
4. Benton, p. 809.
5. Harry Chapman's story.
6. Benton, p. 795.
7. E.R.O., A1001.
8. Benton, p. 834.
9. *Essex Arch. Transactions*, Vol. 9 (1906), pp. 298-300. An excursion on Saturday, 24 September 1904.
10. Benton, p. 795.
11. *Ibid.*
12. Benton, p. 834.
13. *Ibid.*
14. *Ibid.*
15. Pigot's *Directory*, 1835.
16. White's *Directory*, 1848.

17. E.R.O., A1001.
18. D. Smith, *Pigeon Cotes and Dove Cotes of Essex*, Vol. 2 (1931), pp. 130, 131.
19. *Ibid.*
20. *Ibid.*
21. Sir Alfred Temple's *Book of Poems* (1926) (S.R.L.).
22. Benton, p. 796.

Chapter Four

1. J. Weever, *Funereal Monuments* (1631).
2. R. S. Charnock, *Ancient Manorial Customs* (1870).
3. W. H. Black, *A Lawless Court* (R.A.S.).
4. W. Andrews, *Bygone Essex*, pp. 135-142 (1892).
5. Benton, p. 839.
6. Benton, p. 838.
7. E.R.O., D/DCf M25.
8. E.R.O., D/DU183/11.
9. E.R.O., D/DCf M25.
10. Benton, p. 840.
11. E.R.O., D/DQs184/1-10;
12. P. Morant, *A History of Essex*, Vol. 1, p. 272 (1768).
13. P.O. *Directory* (1870).
14. Kelly's *Directory* (1886).
15. Story by Cyril Smoothy, Stambridge Road, Rochford.
16. E.R.O., T/P183/1-6.
17. *Royal Commission on Historical Monuments in Essex*, Vol. 4. p. 130 (1916-23).
18. Documents loaned by Mrs. F. D. B. Shillan, Southend.
19. *Ibid.*

Chapter Five

1-5. Rochford Council Minute Books.
6. Story by 'Chick' Robinson, East Street, Rochford.
7. E.R.O., T/P181/9/14.
8. Story by Cyril Smoothy.

Chapter Six

1. Benton, p. 852.
2. Benton, p. 853.
3. Coller, *op. cit.*, p. 5.

4. Arthur Young, *Agriculture in Essex*, pp. 20, 21 (1813).
5. J. Chamberlayne, *Magnae Britanniae Notitea* (1736).
6-9. Benton, p. 794.
10. Benton, p. 785.
11. E.R.O., Q/SBb269.
12. Appendix to second *Annual Report of Poor Law Commission*, p. 250 (1836).
13. P.O. *Directory* (1876).
14. Kelly's *Directory* (1882).

Chapter Seven
1. E.R.O. T/P181/9/14.

Chapter Eight
1. Benton, p. 854.
2. P. Muilman, *A New and Complete History of Essex*, Vol. 5, p. 273 (1771).
3. Duncan Moul and P. E. Hall, *Picturesque Essex*, p. 182 (1915).
4. Benton, p. 856.
5. P. Muilman, *op. cit.*, p. 173.
6. Benton, p. 858.
7. E.R.O., D/P129/5/2.
8. Benton, p. 858.
9. Pigot's *Directory* (1832).
10. Benton, p. 859.
11. E.R.O., D/AEM2/8.
12. *Royal Commission on Historical Monuments in Essex*, Vol. 4, p. 127 (1916-23).
13. E.R.O., D/CF11/8.
14. E.R.O., D/CC21/4.
15. E.R.O., T/P181/9/14.
16. E.R.O., D/CC21/4.
17. Benton, p. 859.
18. *Additions to Newcourt's Repertorium*, notes by J. Challenor Smith, Vol. 2, p. 112 (1898-1900).
19. P. H. Reany, *Early Essex Clergy*, reprinted from *Essex Review*, Vols. 49--55, p. 138 (1947).
20. As No. 18.
21. E.R.O., D/DQs113/8.
22. Benton, p. 853.

References 177

23. E.R.O., Q/CR3/1/225.
24. E.R.O., D/CT 291A/B.
25. E.R.O., Q/CR3/1/211.
26. *Essex Almanac*, 1872.
27. Information from S. J. Thorn, Secretary, Union of Evangelical Churches.
28. Information from L. W. Kinsey, 43 Hill Road, Chelmsford.
29. E.R.O. T/P181/9/4.

Chapter Nine
1. Benton, p. 897.
2. D. Glennie, *Our Town*, p. 8 (1947) (S.R.L.).
3. Benton, p. 899.

Chapter Ten
1. Diary of Dr. Asplin in Colchester Reference Library.
2. E.R.O., D/DCw M171.
3. Robson's *Commercial Directory* (1839).
4. E.R.O., T/P83/5.
5. E.R.O., D/AEM2/4.
6. P.O. *Directory* (1845).
7. E.R.O., T/Z13/15;
8. E.R.O., E/N1-3;
9. J. Francis, *Recollections* (1916) (R.A.S.).
10. P.O. *Directory* (1859).
11. Kelly's *Directory* (1862).
12. E.R.O., D/AEM2/8.
13. E.R.O., E/N1/22.
14. Information from Brigadier R. Bryers, 'Old Rectory', Eye, Suffolk (Feb. 1968).
15. Prince Chula's *Brought up in England* (1943).

Chapter Eleven
1. *Essex Almanac* (1903).
2. *Essex Almanac* (1909).
3. E.R.O. A1001.
4. E.R.O., B2374.
5. E.R.O., T/P181/9-14.
6. Rochford Council Minutes Book.
7. D. Smith, *Essex Windmills*, Vol. 2, p. 33 (1932).

Chapter Twelve
1. A. F. J. Brown, *Essex at Work*, p. 63 (1969).
2. *Ibid.*, p. 65.
3. *Universal British Directory* (1793) (hereafter abbreviated to *U.B.D.*)
4. E.R.O., D/P129/17/1-9.
5. Pigot's *Directory* (1828).
6. E.R.O., B2365.
7. Pigot's *Directory* (1835).
8. Kelly's *Directory* (1862).
9. Story of Duncan McBryer, Rochford Garden Way, Rochford.
10. Story from, and papers loaned, by P. Whittingham, Ashingdon Road, Rochford.
11. *Ibid.*
12. Story by J. Topsfield, Rochford Garden Way, Rochford.
13. *U.B.D.* (1793).
14. Story by S. C. Harris, former clerk of Rochford Council.
15. W. J. Francis, *Reminiscences* (1926) (R.A.S.).
16. Story by Harry Chapman.

Chapter Thirteen
1. Pigot's *Directory* (1832).
2. P.O. *Directory* (1859).
3. Jabez Francis, *Recollections* (1916), (R.A.S.).
4. Story by W. H. Turner, Rochford.
5. Rochford Union Minute Book (S.R.L.O.) (abbreviated hereafter to R.U.M.B.).
6. Kelly's *Directory* (1851).
7. E.R.O., D/CT291A/B.
8. *Ibid.*
9. *U.B.D.* (1793).
10. E.R.O., D/P129/17/1-9.
11. Benton, p. 878.
12. W. J. Francis, *Reminiscences*.
13. E.R.O., D/DCw M171.
14. E.R.O., T/Z64.
15. *U.B.D.* (1793).
16. E.R.O., D/P129/5/2.
17. R.U.M.B.
18. E.R.O., D/AER34.

References

19. *Southend and Westcliff Graphic*, 3 June 1910.
20. E.R.O., B2365.

Chapter Fourteen
1. E.R.O., P/RR1/3.

Chapter Fifteen
1. E.R.O., Q/RTh5.
2. E.R.O., 124/ER/23.
3. E.R.O., Q/SR356/43.
4. E.R.O., ASS/35/96/24.
5. E.R.O., ASS/35/112/3/97.
6. E.R.O., ASS/35/113/3/65.
7. E.R.O., ASS/35/114/3/23.
8. T/B35/2/2-3.
9. *Ibid.*
10. F. G. Emmison, *Elizabethan Life—Disorder* (1970) (abbreviated hereafter to *Eliz. Life*).
11. *Eliz. Life*, p. 195.
12. *Eliz. Life*, p. 99.
13. *Eliz. Life*, p. 247.
14. *Eliz. Life*, p. 82.
15. *Eliz. Life*, p. 166.
16. E.R.O., D/P129/18/11.
17. E.R.O., Q/SBb270/39.
18. E.R.O., D/P129/9.
19. E.R.O., D/P129/18/6.
20. E.R.O., D/P129/10.
21. E.R.O., D/DChT9.
22. *Essex Standard*, 12 March 1841.
23. Benton, p. 879.
24. E.R.O., J/P4/5.
25. Harry Chapman's story.
26. *Southend Standard*, 22 June 1967, articles on Southend Police, by F. Z. Claro.
27. E.R.O., Q/APb9.

Chapter Sixteen
1. Sydney and Beatrice Webb, *English Local Government—Poor Law History*, p. 215 (1927).

2. *Ibid.*, p. 97.
3. *Ibid.*, p. 103.
4. *Ibid.*, p. 109.
5. *Ibid.*, p. 215.
6. E.R.O., D/P129/18/2.
7. E.R.O., D/P129/18/1.
8, 9. E.R.O., D/P129/18/2.
10. E.R.O., D/P129/12/6.
11. E.R.O., D/P129/18/9.
12. *Report of Poor Law Commissioners* (1834), App. B1.
13. R.U.M.B.
14. E.R.O., T/P83/1. p. 187.
15. R.U.M.B.
16. R.U.M.B.
17. R.U.M.B.
18. R.U.M.B.
19. White's *Directory* (1848).
20. R.U.M.B.
21. Poster, printed J. Francis, owned by 'Chick' Robinson, East Street, Rochford.
22. R.U.M.B.
23. E.R.O., D/P129/25/1-3.
24. E.R.O., D/P129/25/2.
25. E.R.O., D/P129/12/1.
26. Harry Chapman's story.

Chapter Seventeen
1. A. F. J. Brown, *Essex at Work*, p. 83 (1969).
2. *U.B.D.* (1793).
3. Pigot's *Directory* (1823/24).
4. Diary of Dr. Ásplin.
5. Pigot's *Directory* (1832).
6. *Ibid.* (1835, 1839).
7. Robson's *Directory* (1839).
8. Pigot's *Directory* (1832).
9. Pigot's *Directory* (1835).
10. R.U.M.B.
11. P.O. *Directory* (1845).
12. White's *Directory* (1848).
13. P.O. *Directory* (1859).

References

14. Kelly's *Directory* (1851).
15. P.O. *Directory* (1870).
16. P.O. *Directory* (1874).
17. Kelly's *Directory* (1882).
18. Pigot's *Directory* (1867).
19. P.O. *Directory* (1874).
20. P.O. *Directory* (1878).
21. Kelly's *Directory* (1882).
22. Documents of P. Watts, St. Andrews Road, Rochford (D. Harvey, his grandfather).
23. *Essex Review*; G. O. Rickwood, *Essex Posting Houses in 1822*, p. 89.
24. Letter from Divisional Manager, British Railways, Eastern Region, 22 April 1968.
25. Hugh Bodey, *Roads*, p. 33 (1971).
26. N. P. Bray, *Transport and Communications*, p. 11 (1968).
27. L. A. G. Strong, *The Rolling Road*, p. 49 (1956).
28. Benton, p. 785.
29. A. Young, *Agriculture in Essex*, p. 384 (1807).
30. Benton, pp. 785/6.
31. G. A. Cooke, *Topographical Description of Essex*, pp. 105, 106 (1807).
32. *Roads*, p. 401, by Lieut.-Col. D. Peterson, ed. by Edward Mogg (1822).
33. E.R.O., Q/RUt2/8.
34. *Ibid.*
35. Rochford Urban District Council Minute Book (abbreviated hereafter to R.U.D.C.M.B.).
36. *Southend Antiquarian and Historical Transactions*, Vol. 3, No. 4 (1939). 'Southend 1760-1860', by William Pollitt, p. 224.
37. Hugh Bodey, *Roads*, p. 224 (1971).
38. E.R.O., D/DCwM171.

Chapter Eighteen

1. E.R.O., A1001.
2. Diary of Dr. Asplin.
3. Jabez Francis, *Recollections* (1916) (R.A.S.).
4. W. J. Francis, *Reminiscences* (1926) (R.A.S.).

Chapter Nineteen
1. E.R.O., D/DCW P13.
2. Benton, p. 794.
3. J. R. Smith, *William Wellesley Pole and the Essex Estates of Tylney Long* (1969) (at E.R.O.).
4. E.R.O., D/DCW P13.
5. Benton, p. 842.
6. E.R.O., D/DQs184/1-10.
7. E.R.O., A1001.
8. E.R.O., B4068.
9. E.R.O., A1001.
10. *Ibid.*
11. Benton, p. 847.
12. Benton, p. 843.
13. *Ibid.*
14. Benton, p. 846.
15. E.R.O., *Sage's Collection,* Vol. 13/3.
16. Benton, p. 846.
17. E.R.O., D/DCwM171.
18. Benton, p. 847.
19. E.R.O., B1894.
20. E.R.O., A1034.
21. E.R.O., B2374.
22. *History of Essex,* by P. Morant, Vol. 1, p. 271 (1768).
23. Benton, p. 843.
24. E.R.O., A1033.
25. Benton, p. 847.
26. E.R.O., A611.
27. E.R.O., B3032.
28. E.R.O., A611.
29. *Ibid.*
30. E.R.O., T/P83/2.
31. E.R.O., A1001.

Chapter Twenty
1. *Royal Commission on Historical Monuments in Essex,* Vol. 4, p. 129 (1916-23).;
2. E.R.O., T/P83/1.
3. E.R.O., T/P181/9/14.

References

4. Harry Chapman.
5. R.U.D.C.M.B.
6. *Ibid.*
7. Pigot's *Directory* (1832).
8. E.R.O., D/DCwM171.
9. Harry Chapman's story.
10. E.R.O., Q/SBb270/39.
11. E.R.O., D/P129/17/1-9.
12. E.R.O., T/P181/9/14.
13. R.U.D.C.M.B.
14. J. H. Carson, Archivist, H.M. Customs and Excise, London.
15. E.R.O., D/DE011.
16. Kelly's *Directory* (1882).
17. *U.B.D.* (1793).
18. *Southend County Pictorial*, 29 July 1939.

Chapter Twenty-One.

1. John Hendy, *Early Postmarks of British Isles* (1905).
2. Dendy Marshall, *British Post Office*, p. 273 (1926).
3. P.O.R. Post 9/Riding Work 1791.
4. *U.B.D.* (1793).
5. P.O.R. Post 42/Vol. 10, pp. 31, 44.
6. P.O.R. Post 40/195/1813.
7. P.O.R. Post 40/34/1813.
8. P.O.R. Post 40/195/1813.
9. P.O.R. Post 40/422/1822.
10. P.O.R. Post 40/61/1824.
11. P.O.R. Post 35/2032/1843.
12. Harry Chapman's stories.
13. *Ibid.*

Chapter Twenty-Two

Miss Augusta Tawke, *Recollections* (1913).

Chapter Twenty-Three

1. Benton, p. 899
2. E.R.O., D/DU190/15.
3. *U.B.D.*, 1793.
4. Pigot's *Directory* (1828).

5. Pigot's *Directory* (1832).
6. Pigot's *Directory* (1838).
7. P.O. *Directory* (1845).
8. E.R.O., D/DCf T22/38.
9. E.R.O., D/DCh T39.
10. E.R.O., D/DW T176/1.
11. Pigot's *Directory* (1828).
12. *U.B.D.* (1793).
13. Pigot's *Directory* (1823/24).
14. *Ibid.*
15. E.R.O., D/DCf T22.
16. E.R.O., D/DCwM171.
17. E.R.O., D/OU541/3.
18. Pigot's *Directory* (1823/24).
19. Kelly's *Directory* (1890).
20. E.R.O., D/DB T1522.
21. E.R.O., B4429.
22. Harry Chapman's story.

Chapter Twenty-Four
1. Letter from Rochford Council, 25 January 1973.
2. R.C.M.B.
3. R.C.M.B.
4. R.C.M.B.
5. R.C.M.B.
6. R.C.M.B.
7. R.C.M.B.
8. R.C.M.B.
9. R.C.M.B.
10. R.C.M.B.
11. E.R.O., T/P181/9/14.
12. R.C.M.B.

Chapter Twenty-Five
1. E.R.O., Q/RTh5.
2. Dr. K. H. Burley, *Economic Development of late 17th, early 18th century* (1957).
3. Benton, p. 854.
4. A. F. J. Brown, *Essex at Work* (1969).

References

5. E.R.O., Q/CR2/5/1.
6. E.R.O., D/P129/17/1.
7. E.R.O., D/P129/13/2.
8. E.R.O., D/P128/19/12.
9. E.R.O., D/P129/18/11.
10. David C. Douglas, *English Hist. Docs.*, Vol. 12 (1), p. 780, 1833-74 (1956).
11. Hugh Bodey, *Roads*, p. 37 (1971).

INDEX

Acacia House: 136
Airport: 170
Agriculture: 33
Allens, The: 24, 42, 46-47
Almshouses: 100
Andrews, W.: 23
Ark Lane: 65
Arnold, R.: 1
Arthy, A.J.: 13
Asbey, R.: 32, 37, 76, 84
Ashingdon Road: 4, 6, 69
Asplin, Dr.: 35, 54, 115
Asplin Terrace: 28, 82
Assandune: 3

Back Lane: 11, 29
Bakers, The: 78
Barclays: 52
Banks, The: 51
Banyard, J.: 47, 49
Baptists: 47
Barrack Lane: 78, 154
Barrington: 34, 90, 164
Bartons: 9
Bayne, A.: 2
Beard, G.: 74, 104
Beckwith, E.: 45, 54
Birch: 64, 117
Bishops, The: 71, 117
Blacksmiths: 72
Blatches: 133
Bloomfield, H.: 105
Blue Boar: 154

Boleyn, Anne: 2, 14, 16
Boleyn, Anne, Inn: 157
Bootmakers: 82
Boteler: 40
Bowell, W.: 82
Bradford, W.: 77
Bradley Way: 136
Bray's Lane: 60
Brickfields: 64
Bridges, The: 5-7
Bryers, Rev.: 60
Burgess, J.: 72
Burrows, G.: 72
Butchers: 77

Candlemakers: 75
Carey, A.: 36
Carey's Cottages: 38, 64
Carter, C.: 81
Carter, T.: 28
Chapman, H.: 6, 12, 17, 28, 55, 67,
    80, 82, 86, 156
Chase, Insp.: 39, 92-93
Chula, Prince: 60
Clark, I.: 72
Clarkson, J.: 117
Coaches: 103
Coates, H.: 78
Cock Inn: 156
Codd: 5, 111
Codling Bros.: 72
Coller, D.W.: 1, 8, 14
Cook, F.J.: 24

Index

Coombes Farm: 4, 36, 128
Congregationals: 45
Connaught House: 11-12, 53, 69, 119
Corn Exchange: 11, 140, 151
Cotton, Rev.: 42-43, 161
Court House: 139
Cowlings, The: 71
Cromwell House: 70
Crowe, F.: 32, 84
Custom House: 141

Dalys Road: 57
Danehurst: 60
Davies, G.: 79
Day, J.: 82
Dilcock, A.: 41
Diss, M.: 75-76
Dissmore, A.: 78, 165
Doe, F.: 45
Doggett's Farm: 4, 26, 34-35, 41, 115
Domesday: 4
Dovecot: 19
Drapers, The: 70
Durrant: 10

East Street: 4, 25, 36, 39, 45
Eastwood: 2
Eel Hole: 158
Ekco Works: 169
Enigma House: 138
Evan's Farm: 129

Farms, The: 123
Fernside: 11
Fetherby's: 65
Fir Tree House: 12
Fleming's' Farm: 133
Food Riots: 35
Fragniere: 54

Francis: 32, 58-59, 70, 75, 77, 107, 115, 148
Freeman, J.: 75
Freeman's Cottages: 136
Fuller, S.: 78
Furner, F.: 81

Gardiner, Rev.: 41
Garrood, J.: 29, 71
Gasworks: 39, 63
Gillingham, W.W.: 75, 80
Golden Cross Farm: 130
Golden Lion: 58, 84, 157
Goodman, R.: 72
Gothic Cottage: 52
Grabham, Dr.: 91
Great Brays: 129
Gregsons, The: 12-13, 41, 119
Gridley, A.: 72
Grocers, The: 80
Gusted Hall: 4, 131

Hadleigh: 2
Halsey, Conder: 12
Halsey, E.: 13
Hall Road: 5
Harper, H.: 107, 117
Harriott, J.: 7
Harrington, A.: 101, 107, 119
Harveys, The: 78
Hayward, Rev.: 45, 55
Hawtree, Supt.: 86
Hazel, A.: 85
Heddle, W.: 49
Hedgecocks, The: 84, 135
Histed, T.: 59
Hockley, W.: 70
Hollies, The: 70, 81, 106, 138, 148
Horlock, Mrs.: 136, 160
Horse and Groom: 28, 155
Hospitals, The: 159

Hunt, Mrs.: 86
Hunt, R.T.: 69

Industries: 62
Inns, The: 152
Ironmongers, The: 71
Ironwell Lane: 27

Jackson, E.T.: 51-52
Jackson, Stephen: 41, 89, 126
Joslyn, T.: 101

Kemp, N.: 29, 47
Kernott, W.P.: 46, 51, 120
Kersteman, J.: 7
Kings Head Inn: 23, 37, 92, 154
King's Hill: 23, 58
King's Hill Cottages: 26
Knapping, J.: 48

Lawn, The: 16, 41, 139, 140, 151, 154
Lancaster, W.: 79
Lavenders, The: 12, 52, 54, 119, 137
Lings, The: 71, 79
Little Brays: 29, 60
Lodwick, J.: 7
Long, Tylney: 5, 44, 123
Low, Supt.: 91
Lukers: 158

Mafeking: 38
Mail, The: 143
Maltings, The: 141
Malting Cottages: 141
Malting Villas: 63
Mann, H.: 38-39
Manse, The: 46
Market, The: 4, 6, 8-9

Marlborough Head Inn: 78, 153
Martyrs, The: 13
McBryer, T.: 72
McDurmid, T.: 80
Meeson, W.T.: 12, 63, 101, 113, 126
Merrifield, T.: 97, 127
Mews, The: 51
Mills, J.: 59
Mills, The: 66
Monk, Jonas: 88
Moss, F.: 121
Moot House: 135
Murders, The: 85

National School: 57
Naunton, G.: 81
New England: 132
New Ship Inn: 24, 36, 59, 90, 153
Nixon, Rev.: 135, 155
Noble: 26, 55
Norden, J.: 16
North Street: 5, 45, 48

Offin, T.: 81
Offord, J.: 36
Old Ship Inn: 32, 45, 55, 86, 152
Old Ship Lane: 25, 39, 49, 80
Osborne House: 139

Palmer, W.: 77
Payne, W.: 70
Peculiars, The: 47
Pelhams: 132
Pipehorns: 134
Playle, G.: 79
Police: 88
Police Station: 37, 93
Pond, P.: 57
Popplewell, J.: 57
Population, The: 162

Index

Post, The: 143
Post Office: 143
Potash, The: 62
Potters, The: 80
Presbyterians, The: 44
Priors, The: 24, 66, 118
Prince of Wales Inn: 106, 157
Pritchard: 75
Pump, The: 27
Purdey's Farm: 11

Quy, T.: 71, 107, 136
Quy, W.: 120
Quy's Lane: 29

Railway, The: 105, 130, 147
Rankin: 13, 51
Raymond, G.: 45-46, 69
Raynham, Miss S.: 58-59
Religion: 40
Richardson, T.: 57-58
Roads, The: 108
Robertson: 60
Robinson 'Chick': 29, 84
Roche House: 29, 39
Rochford Hall: 14, 16, 23, 123-25
Rodd, A.: 70
Rome and Bishop: 31-32, 37, 72
Rose and Crown Inn: 82, 93, 155
Roughton, P.: 27, 121
Rutterford, J.: 77, 92

Salmon, T.: 89
Salt Bridge: 5-6, 24, 28, 93
Saddlers, The: 72
Schools, The: 54
Scott, F.: 32, 37
Scratton, T.S.: 51
Searles, The: 78
Shelton, D.: 1

Shelley, E.: 9-10, 80
Shillan, F.: 25-26
Sloman, T.: 66, 77
Smoothy's, The: 24, 25, 105
South Street: 5, 24, 27, 39
Sparrow, H.: 12, 24, 27
Spotland House: 61
Squier: 126
Stagg, T.: 67, 79
Star Inn: 37, 158
Stilwell, A.F.: 29, 64, 101
Stocks, The: 77
Strachan, Capt.: 155
Sunnyside: 11
Sutton Ford Bridge: 7, 150
Swaine, Dr.: 7
Swaine's Farm: 127

Tabor, J.: 9, 16, 19
Tailors, The: 69
Tapes: 134
Tasker: 75
Tawke, A.: 16
Tawke, Miss: 140, 149
Tawke, Mrs.: 41
Temple, A.: 21
Temple, Rev.: 45
Thompson, 'Moll': 28
Thorogood, J.: 49
Three Ashes Inn: 156
Topsfields, The: 68, 74
Turner, Sgt.: 92
Turner, R.: 78
Turner, W.: 77
Turnpike, The: 111
Turnpike Cottage: 112

Union, The: 94
Union Lane: 72

Vanderzee: 12
Ventris: 59
Vernon's Head Inn: 104, 154

Warren, F.: 78
Warren's Garage: 25, 28, 68
Watchmaker's, The: 81
Water: 27
Webster, G.: 77
Weir Pond Road: 5, 25, 32, 36, 45
Welds, The: 6
Wellesley, Long Pole: 115
Wesleyans, The: 46, 48

West: 65
West Street: 5-6, 9, 12, 29, 38
Whispering Post: 23
White Horse Inn: 28, 156
Whittinghams, The: 73
Wilkes: 86
Winterbon, G.: 71, 90
Wise, Rev.: 10-11, 44, 164-65
Wood, G.: 47, 60, 131
Wood, H.: 45
Workhouse, The: 12, 94, 150

Zion Villa: 47